THE STATE OF THE WORLD'S CHILDREN
1988

Oxford University Press, Walton Street,
Oxford OX2 6DP
Oxford New York Toronto Delhi Bombay Calcutta
Madras Karachi Peeling Jaya Singapore Hong Kong
Tokyo Nairobi Dar-es-Salaam Cape Town Melbourne
Auckland and associated companies in Beirut Berlin
Ibadan Nicosia

Oxford is a trade mark of Oxford University Press
Published in the United States by Oxford University
Press, New York

British Library Cataloguing in Publication Data
The state of the world's children 1988.
1. Children—Care and hygiene
613′ 0432 RJ101
ISBN 0-19-261723-0

ISSN 0265-718X

The Library of Congress has catalogued this serial
publication as follows:-
The state of the world's children—Oxford
New York: Oxford University Press for UNICEF v.:ill.;
20cm. Annual. Began publication in 1980.
1. Children—Developing countries—Periodicals. 2.
Children—Care and hygiene—Developing countries—
Periodicals. I. UNICEF.
HQ 792.2.S73 83-647550 362.7′1′091724

UNICEF, UNICEF House, 3 U.N. Plaza, New York,
N.Y. 10017 U.S.A.
UNICEF, Palais des Nations, CH. 1211
Geneva 10, Switzerland.

Cover and design: Miller, Craig and Cocking, Woodstock, U.K.
Charts and tables: Stephen Hawkins, Oxford Illustrators, Oxford, U.K.
Typesetting and Printing: Burgess & Son (Abingdon) Ltd, U.K.

Edited and produced for UNICEF and Oxford University
Press by P & L Adamson, Benson, Oxfordshire, U.K.

THE STATE
OF THE WORLD'S
CHILDREN
1988

James P. Grant
Executive Director of the
United Nations Children's Fund
(UNICEF)

PUBLISHED FOR UNICEF

Oxford University Press

CONTENTS

THE STATE OF
THE WORLD'S CHILDREN

STATISTICS

PANELS

TEXT FIGURES

I

THE STATE OF THE WORLD'S CHILDREN 1988

James P. Grant

A grand alliance for children

Alliances in action

Children and recession

Family knowledge

Partners in the alliance

Support for women

Conclusion

Sources

The under-five mortality rate (U5MR) is the number of children who die before the age of 5 for every 1,000 born alive. This year, it is the U5MR figure which governs the order in which the countries are listed in the statistical tables of The State of the World's Children report.

Figures given for the under-five mortality rates of particular countries, in both the text and statistical tables of this report, are estimates prepared by the United Nations Population Division on an internationally comparable basis, using various sources. In some cases, these may differ from national estimates.

A grand alliance for children

One death in every three in the world is the death of a child under the age of five. And each week that goes by, more than a quarter of a million young children still die, in the developing world, from frequent infection and prolonged undernutrition. Yet in the 1980s so far, despite the difficult economic climate, the limited promotion of new low-cost means of protecting children's lives and growth is already resulting in the saving of nearly 40,000 young lives each week. It has therefore been demonstrated that it is now possible to prevent most child deaths and most child malnutrition by means which any developing nation can afford to begin implementing and which every industrialized nation can afford to support.*

These are the facts which tower over any consideration of the state of the world's children as the 1980s draw towards a close. And they are facts which have as much to say about the quality of children's lives as about the quantity of children's deaths. For the combination of preventable infections and undernutrition, which is the main cause of child deaths, also touches the lives of even larger numbers of children who live on with ill health and poor growth, unable today to develop to their full mental and physical potential, unable tomorrow to fully contribute to the families they will have or the communities in which they will live.

---

* A high rate of child deaths is also one of the main reasons for a high rate of child *births* (see page 23). Reducing under-five deaths would, therefore, also help toward the further slowing down, and eventual stabilization, of population growth.

Amid all the many other difficulties facing the world's children, and amid all the other issues with which UNICEF is actively concerned in over 100 nations of the developing world, the questions of child survival and child development therefore remain paramount, not just because of the sheer scale and severity of the problem but because of the emergence, in our times, of dramatic low-cost possibilities for its solution.

Those new possibilities arise from two converging processes:-

First, it is now known that the major threats to the lives and the normal growth of children can be defeated, in large measure, by informing and supporting parents themselves in such basic and inexpensive actions as getting their children immunized, using oral therapies for diarrhoeal disease, maintaining exclusive breast-feeding in the early months, applying new knowledge about when and how to introduce other foods, recognizing the danger signs of acute respiratory infection, spacing births at least two years apart, enrolling for pre-natal care if possible, and putting into practice the essentials of home hygiene (see pages 31 to 37). If applied, these techniques and this knowledge could drastically reduce – by at least 50% – the quiet carnage of a quarter of a million child deaths each week.

Second, the surge in the communications capacity of virtually all nations over the last ten years has made it possible, for the first time, to put that knowledge and these techniques at the disposal of the great majority of the world's people. Sixty per cent of the developing world's adults can now read and write. Eighty per cent of its children now enrol in school.[1] Radio reaches into a majority of its homes, television into a majority of its communities (fig. 11). Government services now reach, with varying degrees of effectiveness, into almost every community. Two million doctors, 6 million nurses, and many more millions of community health workers are now at work. And tens of thousands of non-governmental organizations, peasant co-operatives, labour unions, employers' associations, political cadres, youth organizations, women's movements, and neighbourhood associations now add up to a breadth and depth of organized resources which could be the means of informing and supporting the majority of the developing world's families in using today's knowledge.

Mobilizing this new capacity therefore represents a major opportunity for the advance of primary health care.* And if the start already made can be accelerated, then the goal of 'Health for All by the year 2000' may still be within reach.

The knowledge road to health

A glance down the list of the major causes of child deaths and child malnutrition in the world of 1987 (fig. 1) shows just how far the world's children could now travel down that 'knowledge road to health':-

○ *Diarrhoea* is the leading cause of child death. But approximately 70% of the more than 4 million children killed by diarrhoeal disease this year could have been saved if all parents had been empowered to use the low-cost breakthrough known as oral rehydration therapy or ORT.**

○ More than 3 million children have been killed in the last twelve months by *measles, tetanus, and whooping cough*, and another 200,000 have been permanently disabled by *polio*. Yet the efforts of the last ten years have made immunization widely available and the lives and limbs of almost all those children could have been spared by a course of vaccination costing approximately $5 per child. What is lacking is an equivalent effort to use today's communications capacity to inform parents everywhere of the urgent need for a full course of vaccinations during pregnancy and the first year of a child's life.

○ *Acute respiratory infections*, mainly pneumonias, have killed a further 2 to 3 million underfives this year. Most of those children could also have been saved, by 50 cents' worth of antibiotics administered by a community health worker with only a few months' training. And most of their parents could have sought out that low-cost help if they had known how to distinguish between a bad cough and a life-threatening lung infection and if the medical establishment in more countries were willing to relinquish its exclusive right to administer antibiotics (see page 37).

○ *Undernutrition* was a contributing cause in perhaps one third of the 14 million child deaths in the world last year. And although not having enough to eat is still a fundamental problem in some of the world's very poorest communities, the major cause of undernutrition in the world

---

* 1988 marks the tenth anniversary of the International Conference on Primary Health Care convened by the World Health Organization (WHO) and UNICEF at Alma-Ata in the Soviet Union. That conference distilled decades of experience into an affordable strategy for achieving 'Health for All by the year 2000' and its principles have since guided UNICEF in its search for low-cost and widely applicable methods of protecting the lives and the growth of the world's most vulnerable children.

** Oral rehydration therapy is the name given to a range of actions designed to prevent and treat dehydration, during episodes of diarrhoea, by giving a child fluids by mouth. When a child has diarrhoea, dehydration can often be prevented by giving the child plenty of water and liquids to drink. Better still, the child can be given an oral rehydration solution which parents can make up from sugar, salt, and water in the right proportions. Several traditional remedies such as vegetable or cereal soups and rice conjees are also effective in preventing the onset of dehydration. If the diarrhoea persists and the child begins to become dehydrated, then specially formulated oral rehydration salts (ORS) should ideally be given. ORS too can be administered by parents, after some initial instruction from a health worker. Increasingly available from health centres and pharmacies, ORS costs only a few cents and is the most effective treatment for dehydration (it is now becoming standard procedure in the most up-to-date Western hospitals). In a very small proportion of cases, intravenous rehydration therapy will still be necessary.

Fig. 1 Annual under-five deaths, developing countries, 1987*

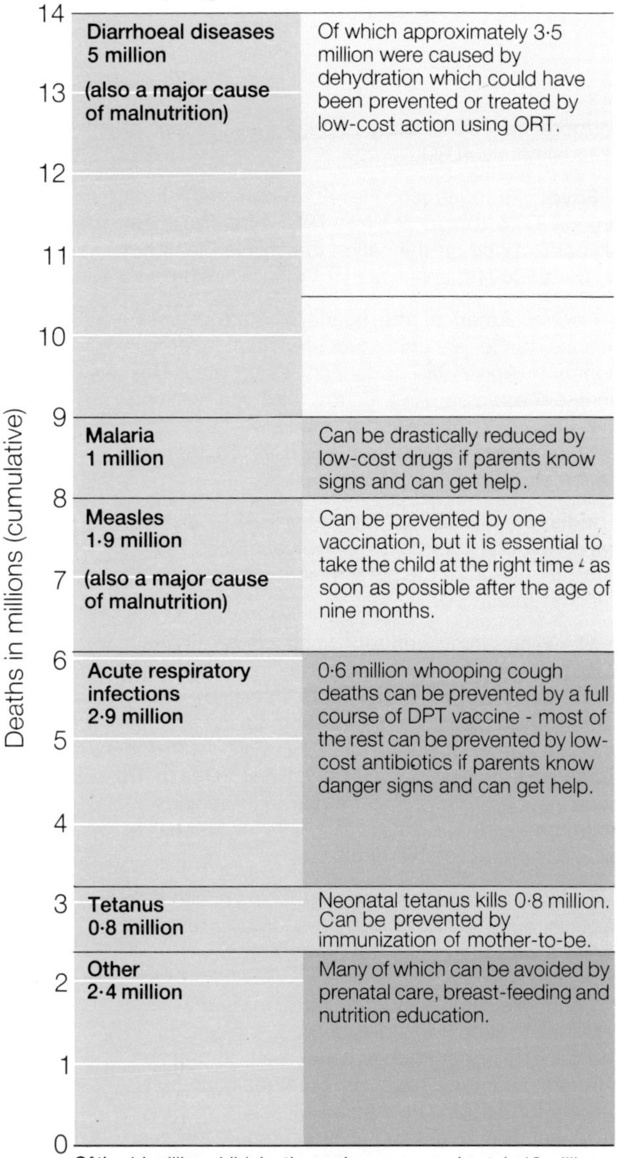

Deaths in millions (cumulative)

14 — 13 — 12 — 11 — 10 — 9 — 8 — 7 — 6 — 5 — 4 — 3 — 2 — 1 — 0

Diarrhoeal diseases **5 million** (also a major cause of malnutrition)	Of which approximately 3·5 million were caused by dehydration which could have been prevented or treated by low-cost action using ORT.
Malaria **1 million**	Can be drastically reduced by low-cost drugs if parents know signs and can get help.
Measles **1·9 million** (also a major cause of malnutrition)	Can be prevented by one vaccination, but it is essential to take the child at the right time – as soon as possible after the age of nine months.
Acute respiratory infections **2·9 million**	0·6 million whooping cough deaths can be prevented by a full course of DPT vaccine - most of the rest can be prevented by low-cost antibiotics if parents know danger signs and can get help.
Tetanus **0·8 million**	Neonatal tetanus kills 0·8 million. Can be prevented by immunization of mother-to-be.
Other **2·4 million**	Many of which can be avoided by prenatal care, breast-feeding and nutrition education.

Of the 14 million child deaths each year approximately 10 million are from only four major causes and all are now susceptible to effective low-cost actions by well-informed and well-supported parents.

*For the purposes of this chart, one cause of death has been allocated for each child death when, in fact, children die of multiple causes and malnutrition is a contributory cause in approximately one third of all child deaths.

Source: WHO and UNICEF estimates.

today is not a shortage of food in the home. It is rather a lack of basic services and a shortage of information about preventing infection and using food to promote growth.* Making sure that all parents know that they can protect their children's nutritional health by such means as birth spacing, care in pregnancy, breast-feeding, immunization, preventing illness, special feeding during and after illness, regularly checking their child's weight gain – and supporting parents in putting that knowledge into action – can overcome most, though not all, cases of malnutrition and poor growth in the world today.

○ A contributing factor in at least one quarter of all today's child deaths is the *timing of births*. Births which are 'too many or too close' to mothers who are either 'too young or too old' carry a very much higher risk for both mother and child (see page 33). Using this knowledge, and today's low-cost means of timing births, is therefore one of the most powerful and least expensive of all levers for raising the level of both child survival and child development.

○ Similarly, more than half of all illness and death among children is associated with inadequate *hygiene*. In communities without safe water supply and sanitation, it is obviously very difficult to prevent the contamination of food and water. But there are low-cost methods which can help to reduce the spread of germs. And all families have a right to know what those methods are (see page 37).

In sum, most child *malnutrition*, as well as most child *deaths*, could now be prevented by parental actions which are almost universally affordable based on knowledge which is already available.

* Malnutrition can be caused by too many births too close together, by the poor nutritional health of the mother resulting in low birth-weight, by infection during pregnancy, by bottle-feeding rather than breast-feeding, by introducing additional foods too early or too late, by ceasing breast-feeding too soon or too suddenly, and by feeding too infrequently and with bulky staples which a child cannot eat enough of to satisfy its energy needs. But the most important cause of all is the frequency of infections, especially diarrhoeal disease and measles, which can reduce the appetite and the intake and absorption of food.

Immunization: a progress report

The success of the smallpox eradication programme in the mid-1970s inspired the World Health Organization to put an even more ambitious objective on the human agenda – immunization of all children against six diseases which were then claiming over 4.5 million young lives each year. That goal was to be achieved by the end of 1990.* A progress report:-

Two thirds of the developing world's children are now receiving a first dose of DPT vaccine and 50% are completing the full course of three injections. Half are also being immunized against polio and 39% against measles. The result is the saving of approximately 1.4 million young lives each year.

If the present momentum can be maintained, then 1990 will see immunization coverage in the developing world reaching almost 75% for DPT and almost 70% for measles (figures include China). The target is therefore within range for the majority of developing countries – and could be reached by an acceleration of the effort over the next three years.

No country faces inevitable failure to meet the target. Nations like Colombia and Turkey have recently shown that immunization levels can be dramatically raised in a short space of time if the whole of society is mobilized to achieve it. Influenced by such examples, over 80 nations have recommitted themselves to the 1990 goal and reaccelerated their efforts to reach it. Those countries include the 30 most populous nations of the developing world. Some examples of the recent surge:-

Senegal: coverage has been lifted from very low levels to approximately 70% in one year (panel 2).

Syria: immunization against the six major vaccine-preventable diseases has been lifted from 25% in 1985 to 70% in 1987 (panel 3).

Pakistan: an Accelerated Health Programme has pushed immunization coverage from 3% in 1981 to more than 55% today (though measles lags at approximately 40%).

Egypt: immunization levels have risen from around 50% to over 80% in 1987 after President Mubarak called on the nation to achieve the target by the thirty-fifth anniversary of the revolution.

Central America: the heads of state of seven nations made an unprecedented joint television appeal in April 1987 to launch 'Vaccination Day' across the region. And for the third year running, the Church in **El Salvador** mediated cease-fires between government and guerrillas so that the nation's children could be immunized.

India: Nearly 200 of the nation's 420 districts have now been covered in a five-year $750 million effort to immunize the great majority of the nation's children (panel 10).

Many problems confront such efforts. Turkey, Pakistan, and Brazil are struggling to maintain the levels achieved in recent years (panel 9). Many nations also seem to be coming up against an invisible barrier at about the 70% mark – with the urban poor proving particularly difficult to reach. In most nations, measles coverage lags behind despite the fact that measles accounts for over half of all vaccine-preventable deaths.

The way forward lies in strengthening health care facilities and mobilizing every resource to reach all families with the immunization message.

---

*In principle, 'universal immunization' is that level required to stop transmission of EPI diseases, in the country or community concerned. In practice, different countries have set different quantitative targets for 1990. The African Ministers of Health have set the target at 75% coverage for each antigen. China is aiming at 85% coverage in each province by 1988 and in each county by 1990. Where countries have not yet set their own quantitative target for 1990, UNICEF uses 80% coverage for each antigen as a minimum indication of universal immunization being achieved. The 1990s should see higher levels of coverage.

Informing and facilitating such parental action is therefore the major challenge of child health today.

A revolution beginning

Five years ago, when UNICEF first articulated this potential for a revolution in child survival and development, it was argued that the use made of new knowledge depended almost entirely on social organization. Health promotion is the great need and the great opportunity of our times. But it is not the exclusive responsibility of, and cannot be accomplished by, the health services alone. By and large, those health services cannot reach out far enough or often enough to bring about change in knowledge and behaviour on the necessary scale. Nor are they either staffed or trained for the task of empowering millions of people to protect their own and their families' health. The expertise and guidance of the medical profession is essential, but it remains a profession which is better equipped to respond to illness rather than to promote health.

Therefore if the challenge is to be met, it will be met by a social movement rather than by a medical movement alone. And what is needed is a society-wide alliance of all those who could communicate with and support parents in doing what can now be done – teachers and religious leaders, mass media and government agencies, voluntary organizations and people's movements, business and labour unions, professional associations and conventional health services. Only such a Grand Alliance for Children can create the informed public demand for, and practical knowledge of, those methods which could bring about the revolution in child survival and development.

Today that Grand Alliance has begun to gather. And the child survival and development revolution is now under way.

Immunization coverage, for example, has extended its reach from less than 10% to approximately 50% of the developing world's children during the 1980s (fig. 4). As a result, vaccines are now estimated to be saving the lives of approximately 1.4 million children each year. Similarly,

ORT, which was largely unknown outside the scientific community at the beginning of this decade, is now being used by approximately 20% of the world's families and preventing an estimated 600,000 dehydration deaths each year among the world's young children.

Taken together, immunization and ORT are therefore now saving the lives of approximately 2 million children each year. As the Secretary-General of the United Nations has said: *"a veritable child survival revolution has begun to spread across the world"*.

But it is only a beginning. And the essential task now is to broaden and deepen that Grand Alliance for Children in order to fully realize the potential which has been so clearly demonstrated.

Sadly, the 1980s have also seen counter-currents running against such progress for the world's children. The weight of wars and conflict in many parts of Africa (panel 17), and of armed conflict in Central America and between Iraq and Iran, has fallen most heavily on the children of those regions. Less visible but just as tragic has been the economic recession which, in recent years, has eroded both family incomes and government services in so many nations of the developing world. Pages 23 to 31 of this report summarize the impact of that recession on children and outline UNICEF's response – the call for 'adjustment with a human face'.

Briefly, the challenge is one of adjusting economies to recession and restoring economic growth while at the same time shielding the most vulnerable families, and especially the growing minds and bodies of their children, from the worst effects of a necessary economic austerity. And paradoxically, that context of crisis provides a special opportunity to promote, on a massive scale, such measures as immunization and ORT, breast-feeding and birth spacing, better weaning and regular growth monitoring. For these are the very measures which can offer the most protection for the least cost to the largest number of children. Yet they are also measures which can be afforded even in difficult economic times – *if* a nation's leaders make a clear political commitment to that goal and *if* a nation's organized resources form a grand alliance to achieve it.

Senegal: showing it can be done

2

In 1985, fewer than 10% of Senegal's children were immunized and vaccine-preventable diseases were killing 30,000 children a year. Today, approximately 70% are protected against TB, diphtheria, whooping cough, tetanus, polio, measles, and yellow fever.

The fact that Senegal is among the 30 poorest nations in the world means that its example is as important as its achievement. For Senegal has shown that there is no nation which cannot immunize the great majority of its children by the UN target date of 1990 – if political leaders are committed to it and if social and economic resources are mobilized to achieve it.

Senegal, like most African countries, cannot rely on television to reach more than 20% of the population. Literacy is low and newspapers are read by only a small, mainly urban, audience. Radio is the only modern medium capable of reaching the majority of parents.

To overcome these handicaps, a very wide range of less conventional channels – including traditional means of communication – were mobilized.

In October 1986, President Diouf asked every government ministry and all sections of society to join in an effort to immunize 75% of Senegal's young children by World Health Day – 7 April 1987.* "Vaccination," he announced, "is everybody's business."

Soon afterwards a special national committee, representing a cross-section of society, took charge of the most ambitious immunization programme ever mounted in Africa. In each region, department, and urban neighbourhood, similar committees were formed. All ranks of the civil service were involved.

Radio played a key role in informing parents about the benefits of immunization – through news reports, advertising spots, interviews, feature programmes, and specially composed plays, poems, and stories. The press and television reached a small but influential audience.

But the distinctive feature of Senegal's achievement was the massive use of traditional communications to inform and encourage parents. Throughout the country, neighbourhood heads and local council members held meetings or visited parents at home. In mosques, imams urged parents to have their children vaccinated. Thousands of *griots* – traditional story-tellers and messengers – beat the drums to announce the arrival of the immunization teams.

Women's organizations held meetings to ensure that children were brought to vaccination posts. Tens of thousands of schoolchildren, Boy Scouts and Girl Guides also went from house to house, making immunization lists and informing parents of the time and place of the nearest vaccination session. Youth and sports organizations held concerts, football games, and traditional wrestling matches, with parades of children wearing T-shirts with the slogan '*Vaccination for all children*'.

But merely creating the demand would not have been enough. The health services also achieved a remarkable feat by making vaccination available on a routine basis at all the nation's 650 health centres and health posts. Mobile teams travelled great distances over rough terrain so that no parent would have to bring a child more than 5 kilometres.

To make vaccination even more accessible, communities set up temporary posts in mosques, schools, private homes, or under a shady tree in the village square. Trade unions and political parties organized vaccination sessions in offices, factories, and homes.

Senegal's triumph demonstrates how a low-income country can mobilize its human resources to increase demand for, and access to, immunization. It also opens up new horizons for other child health strategies, such as the control of malaria, respiratory infections, and diarrhoeal disease, as well as birth spacing, and growth promotion

* The target is 80% by World Health Day 1988.

As the 1990s approach, that commitment to children is beginning to be made.

The gathering alliance

As previous editions of this report have described in more detail, nations such as Colombia and Turkey, Syria and Senegal, Pakistan and India, Brazil and Bolivia, Egypt and Ecuador, Thailand and Bangladesh, have saved literally millions of young lives during the 1980s by doubling or trebling immunization coverage, by making ORT available to parents, by promoting breast-feeding, and by monitoring child growth.

In each of these examples, the rapid spread of basic health knowledge and low-cost techniques has been made possible by continuing society-wide alliances involving some combination of political and religious leaders, teachers and students, mass media and traditional information channels, trade unions and employers, village leaders and local councils, youth organizations and women's movements, professional associations and voluntary organizations.

Internationally also, an informal alliance for children is beginning to coalesce. In 1987, for example, seven heads of state in Central America have made an unprecedented joint television appeal for the immunization of all children as part of a new programme to halve child death rates in the region. In Asia, the seven heads of state of the South Asian Association for Regional Co-operation (SAARC) have jointly stated that "*children should be given the highest priority in national development planning*" (panel 15). Similarly, African heads of state meeting in Addis Ababa have declared 1988 a "*year for the protection, survival, and development of the African child*" and urged all African nations to achieve universal immunization by 1990 as a step toward primary health care.

Growing support is also coming from several industrialized nations. The government of *Italy*, for example, has allocated over $130 million to assist 35 nations (26 of them in Africa) in reaching the target of universal immunization by 1990. Similarly, the *United States* Congress has allocated over $150 million to a special Child Survival Fund – including approximately $90 million for the promotion of immunization and ORT.[2] The governments of *Canada* and *Sweden*, with widespread public support, have also allocated $100 million and $50 million respectively to help accelerate the spread of immunization coverage across the developing world. In support of UNICEF's child survival efforts, the governments of *Norway* and *Finland* have also significantly increased their financial commitments.*

One non-governmental organization – Rotary International – was among the first to make a major commitment to this cause and is now drawing close to its target of raising $120 million for polio vaccination programmes world-wide.

Accelerating the momentum

With support from many leaders of the world's religious orders, international non-governmental organizations, leading associations of medical professionals, and the media of many nations, the Grand Alliance for Children is beginning to coalesce around the cause of putting today's low-cost child protection methods at the disposal of the vast majority of parents. Two million lives a year are already being saved by this process, and the goal of reducing the 1980 levels of child deaths and child malnutrition by at least half in the remaining years of this century is now demonstrably achievable.

Now is not the time, therefore, to change the goal or diffuse the effort. Many other problems of

---

* Both as forum and as participant, the United Nations is also making a crucial contribution to this cause. To mark the fortieth anniversary of the United Nations in 1985, and in answer to the Secretary-General's call, over 70 governments and more than 400 voluntary organizations have signed a Declaration of renewed commitment to the goal of immunization for all children by the year 1990. A year earlier, several United Nations agencies, the World Bank, and the Rockefeller Foundation formed the international Task Force for Child Survival, which has since played an important part in promoting immunization and other basic child protection measures in the developing world. Next year (1989) should also see the presentation to the UN General Assembly of a new Convention on the Rights of the Child, dealing with a wide range of children's problems (panel 16).

children cry out for attention and action. But a world-wide consensus is growing that the greatest of human tragedies – the frequent infection, poor growth, and early death of so many of the world's children – can be dramatically reduced in our times. And practical progress towards that goal is gathering momentum.

Therefore the task of the hour is to accelerate that momentum. And if the great goal of ensuring these, the most basic of our children's rights, can be achieved by such an alliance, then it may be that a powerful force will also have been created for achieving other rights and more effectively tackling other problems – the problems of children who are disabled or retarded, children who are abandoned or neglected, children who live in refugee camps or on the streets of cities, children who are victimized by war or exploited at work, children in the grip of drugs or alcohol, children who suffer violence or sexual abuse, and children who lack education, water, or food.

That alliance for that goal is therefore the central theme of this year's *State of the World's Children* report. And not by coincidence, it is a theme summed up by the slogan which the World Health Organization (WHO) has chosen for its fortieth anniversary year in 1988 – 'Health for All – All for Health'.

As a contribution to that cause, this report constitutes a direct appeal for the involvement of all possible resources in an alliance for child health. For today, there is hardly an individual or organization, in either industrialized or developing worlds, that cannot help to fight for the survival and healthy development of all the world's children by informing and supporting parents in applying what is now known.

There is therefore hardly an individual or organization that will not find, in the pages of this year's *State of the World's Children* report, a challenge to practical involvement, a bottom line of action, a part to play in the Grand Alliance for Children.

Alliances in action

The gathering alliance for children is also part of a wider struggle for primary health care. And today, one of the common strands in that struggle is that for all ages, and in all nations, the broadest way forward lies in informing and supporting families everywhere in putting already available knowledge into practice.

A brief look at the major threats to the life and health of *adults*, world-wide, will illustrate that world-wide theme.

The leading causes of serious illness and death among adults are cancer and heart disease. Yet their toll could now be cut by perhaps as much as 50% or more through people's own well-informed decisions on smoking, diet, and exercise. Simi-

larly, alcohol-related accidents and illnesses are among the leading causes of premature death in most nations, yet the solution to this major health problem also lies in the hands of the informed individual rather than the medical professional. And to this list of major health threats must now be added AIDS. For although the number of AIDS-related deaths in the last twelve months is probably less than the number of deaths from diarrhoeal dehydration in the last 48 hours, the AIDS virus could claim the lives of anywhere between 5 and 30 million adults and children over the decade ahead.[3] And at this stage, the most effective weapon the world has against this new threat is public education to empower people with the knowledge to defend themselves and their families by their own decisions and actions.

In the industrialized world, there is growing evidence that this opportunity may be taken at the flood. Despite the expenditure of approximately $2 billion a year in advertising by the tobacco industry, for example, some 33 million Americans are now ex-smokers (fig. 2). The result has been a 39% fall in heart disease between 1963 and 1984. Similarly, the Soviet Union has recently launched a $500 million public education campaign designed to raise levels of human health and productivity by 'self-health' action to improve diets and reduce alcohol consumption. And in the two years since the Soviet leadership decided to mobilize communications and legislative capacity against alcohol abuse, consumption is reported to have dropped by approximately 50%.[4]

Panels 4 and 14 briefly summarize the steps which can be and are being taken in the industrialized world to empower people with self-health knowledge. Overall, it is clear that the potential of this approach is much greater than that of any conceivable scientific advance.[5] It is now estimated, for example, that it would take the expenditure of many billions of dollars a year on new medical technology to add just one more year to the average human life expectancy of Europe or North America. By contrast, a full *ten years* could now be added to the life-span of the average male, at low or even no cost, by individual decisions on eating sensibly, exercising regularly, smoking not at all, and drinking alcohol only in moderation.

In the very different circumstances of the developing world, the potential for self-health action is even greater. No conceivable increase in expenditure on medical technology, no amount of building of more hospitals or training of more doctors, could now offer a health return on investment which even begins to compare with the benefits of primary health care strategies designed to inform and support the developing world's parents in using today's knowledge about birth spacing, breast-feeding, immunization, safe weaning, feeding after illness, oral rehydration therapy, domestic hygiene, coping with respiratory infections, and promoting regular weight gain.*

Both industrialized and developing worlds therefore now stand at clearly marked crossroads on the road to health. If the road chosen is the road of primary reliance on medical technology, then the path will become steeper and more difficult, requiring the expenditure of more and more resources for less and less forward progress,

Fig. 2 Percentage of daily smokers, industrialized countries, 1965–1985

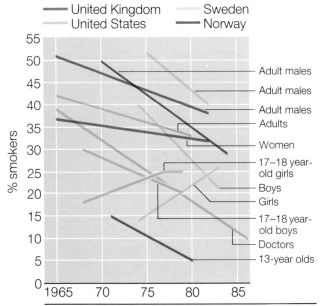

Despite the expenditure of some $2 billion a year to advertise tobacco products, education and legislation is succeeding in reducing tobacco consumption by approximately 1% a year in the industrialized world. In the developing world, consumption is rising by more than 2% a year.

Source: "WHO Programme on Tobacco or Health, Report by the Director-General", WHO, November 1985.

---

* In the industrialized world, the four most important areas for low-cost individual health action are sometimes known by the acronym SAFE – for action on Smoking, Alcohol, Food, and Exercise. In some parts of the developing world, UNICEF and its partners use the acronym GOBI for the four kinds of low-cost family-based health action which have an equivalent power in the protection of the lives and growth of children – Growth promotion, Oral rehydration therapy, Breast-feeding, and Immunization. To these are sometimes added the 'three Fs' of Family spacing, Food supplements, and Female education, which, although more expensive and more difficult to achieve, have been shown to be among the most powerful influences on the survival and normal development of children in poor communities.

Syria: mobilizing to plan

3

In the mid-1980s, infections like measles and whooping cough were killing some 7,000 Syrian children a year and disabling many thousands more. Syria's parents knew and feared these diseases, but most believed there was nothing to be done. Only 25%-30% of children were fully immunized, despite the fact that immunization had been widely available since 1978.

Today, this picture has changed. Most Syrian parents now know what they can do and immunization coverage against measles, polio, diphtheria, whooping cough, tetanus and tuberculosis is close to 70%.

The transformation has been achieved through a remarkable campaign.

Television, radio and newspapers have brought knowledge of immunization into virtually every Syrian home. Hundreds of thousands of booklets, posters, leaflets, stickers, and even bread wrappers have reinforced the message. A million letters have been sent to parents through schools. Tens of thousands of teachers, religious leaders, health workers and volunteers have spoken with parents in homes and places of worship to reassure them about the benefits and the safety of vaccines.

Most of these methods have been used elsewhere. But Syria's special achievement is to have combined them into a systematic national plan involving political leaders, mass media, health professionals and hundreds of other organizations. And it has demonstrated what can now be achieved by planned national mobilization.

That planning began almost a year in advance with the Prime Minister setting up a committee chaired by the Minister of Health. Its members included the Ministries of Information, Education, Religious Affairs, Interior, Defence, Local Administration and Planning, as well as WHO, UNICEF, and the Women's, Peasants', and Youth Unions.

As a first step, surveys found out why most parents had not had their children immunized. Many were simply unaware of the benefits. Some feared side-effects. Others accepted disease as a 'rite of passage' which every child had to undergo.

As a result, 48 messages were designed for use on posters, stickers, radio and TV. Entertainers launched campaign songs which became national hits. A well-known TV personality interviewed mothers for programmes which reached over 90% of the nation.

The campaign reached its peak with the first vaccination week in mid-September 1986. Syria's President vaccinated a baby against polio – drawing nation-wide media coverage and encouraging parents to bring their children. In all, 1,975 vaccination posts were open all day every day (75% of them temporary – in schools, mosques, churches, and community halls).

In the third round the numbers fell, mainly because of the harvest and the bad weather. The government's response was a fourth round, bringing coverage for each vaccine to about 70%.

After such a campaign, it was obvious that here was a strategy which could significantly improve the nation's health in other ways. The Prime Minister soon asked Syrian television for a similar campaign against smoking, with advertisements appearing daily in early 1987.

The campaign has also raised the possibility of empowering parents with other child health knowledge. A permanent Health Education Committee, drawn from a cross-section of government and society, has just been established.

Within Syrian Television, a Health Education Unit has been set up under the leadership of the popular presenter who did so much to promote the immunization campaign.

"Our next campaign," says the Committee's Chairman, "will be combating diarrhoea, followed by promoting breast-feeding, and maintaining high immunization.

"In Syria, television is a service provided by the government, like education. The information media have great power, so they must also assume great responsibility, especially for the health of the nation's children."

and allowing fewer and fewer people to pass through a narrowing valley of ever-increasing cost. If, on the other hand, we choose the road of primary reliance on empowering people with the knowledge to take more control over their own health and facilitating the use of that knowledge, then the way will broaden out to allow the great majority of the human family to move forward towards the goal of health for all.

Knowledge and poverty

For all the new horizons it may lead to, the knowledge road to health will be neither smooth nor downhill. Nor will progress along it be in any way automatic.

In practice, knowledge is only one strand in the pattern of human behaviour. And in many communities today, the power of the informed individual to take more control over family health is a power often circumscribed by poverty, dimmed by lack of education, frustrated by the unequal status of women, muddied by the propaganda of commercial vested interests, and limited by the availability of such basic physical prerequisites as clean water, safe sanitation, and adequate housing.

That is why the empowering of individuals to provide for their own health can never be a substitute for government action to facilitate that process by providing basic community services, guaranteeing a fair return for a family's labour, enacting land reforms, and building up the vital infrastructure of primary health care. Nor should the encouragement of individual responsibility for health be allowed to detract in any way from the international community's responsibility for helping to end the poverty and injustice which remain the fundamental cause of most illness and premature death in the world today.

Over time, of course, advances on both these fronts are mutually reinforcing. Any improvement in the mental and physical development of children contributes fundamentally to the social and economic development of nations. Similarly, any economic development increases the capacity of both nations and families to protect the lives and the normal growth of their children. But a constant theme of the development story over the last forty years is that there is no fixed relationship between a given level of development and the well-being of the poorest sections of a society. At *any* level of development, if the poorest and most vulnerable are to benefit in times of economic progress or to be protected in times of economic hardship, then there has to be a conscious national effort to fashion available resources into a shield against the worst aspects of poverty and ill health.

Given today's new knowledge and new communication capacity, the potential for protecting the poorest is now greater than ever before. And mobilizing to promote available knowledge, and to facilitate its use, now offers what amounts to a change of gear for development, an improvement in the ratio between available resources and social progress.

The major responsibility for this process rests with national governments. And in the not too distant future, those governments will surely come to be judged by whether or not they have eliminated mass child deaths from such basic ills as diarrhoeal dehydration and vaccine-preventable diseases, and whether or not they have empowered their citizens with today's knowledge and provided them with the basic services which allow them to put that knowledge into practice.

There is no conflict here, no 'either/or' between the struggle to change the economic and social status quo and the struggle to improve human well-being within the status quo. Both are always necessary. No-one would seek to deny that poverty is a major cause of malnutrition and ill health among the world's children and that fundamental social and economic change is necessary to end that poverty.

But neither does the analysis of the socio-economic causes of ill health detract for one minute from the right of all families to today's scientific information which could help them to protect the lives and health of their children by methods they can act on *now* and at a cost they can afford *today*.

United States: knowledge for health

4

Putting today's health knowledge into the hands of the public is not a strategy for the developing world alone. Several industrialized nations have also recognized that no other investment can take so many so far down the road to health.

At the beginning of the 1980s, a ten-year programme was launched in the United States to promote information which the government considers all citizens ought to know by the year 1990. Calling on "professionals and lay people alike to use available knowledge ... to reduce preventable death and disease", the US Department of Health has asked the scientific community to sum up that knowledge for use by schools, the mass media, and all other information channels. Some of the goals:-

○ By 1990, the percentage of adults able to state the principal risk factors for coronary heart disease and stroke (high blood pressure, cigarette smoking, elevated blood cholesterol levels, and diabetes) should rise from 11% (the 1979 figure) to at least 50%.

○ By 1990, the share of the adult population aware that smoking is one of the major risk factors for heart disease should be increased to at least 85% (and the proportion of adults who smoke should be reduced from today's 32% to below 25%).

○ By 1990, 50% of the overweight population should have adopted weight-loss regimens combining an appropriate balance of diet and physical activity.

○ By 1990, at least 75% should be able to identify the principal dietary factors known, or strongly suspected, to be related to each of the following diseases: heart disease, high blood pressure, dental caries, and cancer.

○ By 1990, the proportion of adults who can accurately identify the variety and duration of exercise thought to promote cardiovascular fitness most effectively should be greater than 70%.

○ By 1990, 80% of high school seniors should state that they perceive great risk in cigarette smoking, marijuana use, barbiturate use, or alcohol intoxication.

○ By 1990, 85% of women of child-bearing age should be able to choose foods wisely and understand the hazards of smoking, alcohol, pharmaceutical products and other drugs during pregnancy and lactation.

○ By 1990, all mothers of new-borns should receive instructions on immunization schedules for their babies.

○ By 1990, the proportion of women who breastfeed their babies should be increased to 75% at hospital discharge and to 35% at six months of age.

○ By 1990, every high-school student in the United States should receive accurate, timely education about sexually transmitted diseases.

○ By 1990, at least 75% of citizens over fourteen years of age should be able to describe accurately the various contraceptive methods, including their relative safety and effectiveness.

In a mid-term review of progress towards these objectives, the US Assistant Secretary for Health concludes: "We can be extremely pleased at the high level of public awareness about life-style factors and their contribution to health. As people become better informed about the risks of smoking, poor nutritional habits and being overweight, misuse of alcohol and drugs, and inattention to injury-preventing safety measures, personal choices to act on that knowledge are possible, and reductions in related mortality and morbidity will follow. Already we have begun to see such results from reductions in smoking, per capita alcohol consumption, and the increasing use of automobile seat-belts. Already we have noted reduced death rates from strokes, cirrhosis, and traffic accidents. On the other hand, knowledge has not yet preceded healthier behavior in areas such as weight control, illicit drug use, and control of violent behavior."

The alliance of resources which can achieve that goal is potentially the most important social movement of our times. And as the next section will show, this movement is now beginning to come together, in some nations of the world, with some dramatic early results.

Universal immunization by 1990

So far, the main testing grounds of the Grand Alliance for Children have been the attempts to provide immunization and oral rehydration.

There are those who have argued that this focus is too narrow and that ORT and vaccines have been over-emphasized in UNICEF's advocacy over recent years. The reply must be that when the world has at its disposal two of the least expensive and most effective public health techniques of all time, techniques which are capable of defeating both of the greatest threats to the lives and the normal growth of the world's children, then it surely makes sense to give them the highest priority until that job is done. And if we cannot mobilize the will to put these most basic elements of child protection into action for the sake of saving the lives of up to 7 million children each year, at a cost which is negligible for such a cause, then what chance do we realistically have of making significant progress against the plethora of other, often more difficult, problems which face the world's children?

In the last five years, immunization has gathered a new momentum (fig. 3). It is now vital that this momentum be maintained. In the 1980s, just three vaccine-preventable infections – measles, whooping cough, and tetanus – have killed approximately 25 million young children – more than the entire under-five population of the United States or Western Europe. We have the low-cost means to stop that unconscionable carnage and to stop it within the next few years. If we do not now use those means, then our pretensions towards civilization and our hopes of human progress will not stand up to any further examination.

Through the United Nations, the world has set the target of immunizing the great majority of

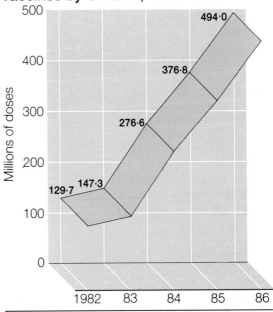

Fig. 3 Increase in the supply of vaccines by UNICEF, 1982–1986*

The world-wide supply of vaccines by UNICEF has increased almost four-fold in four years.
* The chart shows the total supply of all EPI vaccines - BCG, DPT, DT, polio, measles, and TT. Vaccines supplied by UNICEF represent approximately three-quarters of all EPI vaccines supplied to the developing world.
Source: UNICEF and WHO estimates.

children against six main diseases by 1990.* And with whatever tenacity and single-mindedness is necessary, that target must be achieved. If any further incentive were necessary, it should also be mentioned that the creation of a universal system for immunization will be essential to the delivery of new vaccines – for example against malaria and AIDS – which may well be developed over the

* No nation has ever achieved 100% immunization coverage. Developing countries are therefore setting their own targets with 80% being considered a minimum acceptable level (coverage in the industrialized world is just over 70% for DPT and just under 80% for measles and polio). When immunization coverage reaches 80% or more, disease transmission patterns are affected and a degree of protection is conferred on unimmunized children (providing they are distributed evenly and not concentrated in areas with very low immunization coverage).

course of the next decade. Malaria currently kills more than a million people each year. Unchecked, AIDS may become an even greater threat to human life. The actual and potential benefits, to the whole world, of a universal and permanent immunization system are therefore incalculable. The cost of immunization in the developing world, on the other hand, has been calculated at approximately $500 million per year – about the same as ten advanced F-14 fighter aircraft. Building that permanent immunization system therefore represents one of the greatest investment opportunities open to humanity.

Over the last two years, the proportion of the developing world's children covered by DPT vaccine has increased by 7 percentage points a year (fig. 4). Against measles, the average increase has been 8 percentage points a year. Assuming that this average rate of increase is maintained in each nation over the three years between the end of 1987 and the end of 1990, the overall picture will be that 70% or more of the developing world's children will be immunized against diseases which less than a decade ago were killing four to five million children a year.

In other words, if the efforts of recent years can be sustained and accelerated, there is now every chance of achieving one of the most important goals which the world community has ever set for itself.

Present trends also suggest that approximately 30 individual nations will fall short of the 1990 target unless a supreme effort is mounted before the end of the decade. But trends are not inevitabilities. And all nations *could* still achieve and sustain the 1990 target. Dr. Ralph Henderson, the Director of WHO's Expanded Programme on Immunization (EPI), has repeatedly emphasized that "*no committed country with a realistic EPI plan of operations needs to be constrained by a lack of vaccines, cold-chain equipment, or supplies*".[6] The main problem is therefore not finding the vaccines or the syringes or the refrigerators. It is finding the political commitment, finding the management and organizational skills, and finding the ways and means to inform all parents that all pregnant women need to be vaccinated against tetanus and that all children need a *full course* of vaccines before the age of one.*

Universal child immunization therefore depends on mobilizing an alliance of all possible resources to reach out to all parents with information and support.

In theory, vaccination is 'available' now to the great majority of people. But clinics can be far away, transport can be erratic and expensive, queues can be long, vaccination times can be uncertain, other members of the family may say it's not worth it, parents may not know that several vaccinations are necessary and that the timing is important, the child may not be well, and the work in the fields, especially at harvest time, may beckon with more urgency. Unless the reasons for overcoming all these obstacles are made abundantly clear, and unless the times and places of vaccination can be made more convenient, turn-out rates will continue to be low and drop-out rates will continue to be high.[7]

Immunization in the developing world is therefore simply not as easy or automatic as it is for most parents in the industrialized world. And if they are to make the effort to take a child who is not sick to a clinic on three or four separate occasions in the first year of the child's life,** then all parents must be frequently informed, from all possible sources, that a full course of vaccinations is essential to protect the lives and normal growth of their children from some of the most dangerous diseases of childhood.

Immunization is therefore a permanent communications challenge. And there is still a long way to go.

---

* Tetanus, arising from unhygienic birth conditions, kills approximately 800,000 new-borns each year. Two vaccinations with tetanus toxoid during pregnancy, or one booster dose for a previously vaccinated mother, will protect the new-born child until it can be vaccinated in its own right.

** The WHO recommended immunization schedule is as follows: birth – BCG for tuberculosis and the first oral polio vaccination (OPV1); six weeks – the first shot against diphtheria, whooping cough and tetanus (DPT1) and OPV2; ten weeks – DPT2 and OPV3; fourteen weeks – DPT3 and OPV4; nine months – measles.

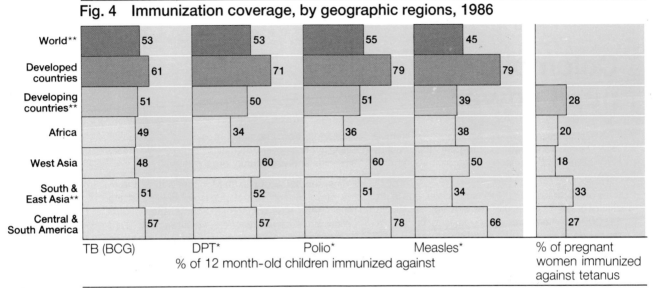

Fig. 4   Immunization coverage, by geographic regions, 1986

	TB (BCG)	DPT*	Polio*	Measles*	% of pregnant women immunized against tetanus
World**	53	53	55	45	
Developed countries	61	71	79	79	
Developing countries**	51	50	51	39	28
Africa	49	34	36	38	20
West Asia	48	60	60	50	18
South & East Asia**	51	52	51	34	33
Central & South America	57	57	78	66	27

% of 12 month-old children immunized against

Half the developing world's infants are now being immunized with BCG, diptheria, pertussis, tetanus and poliomyelitis vaccines before the age of 12 months; 39% are being immunized against measles. 28% of pregnant women in developing countries are immunized against tetanus.

Source: WHO, UNICEF and U.N. Population Division.

*In some countries DPT and polio vaccinations are given for 2 doses only and measles vaccinations are given after 12 months.
**Excluding China, where recent surveys in 28 provinces showed coverage rates of 70% for BCG, 62% for DPT, 68% for polio, and 63% for measles.

But, in the last two years, the strategy of social mobilization has again shown that it can achieve remarkable results even in the face of previous pessimism and present economic problems:-

◯ *Syria* has more than doubled its immunization coverage between the beginning of 1985 and the end of 1986, so saving more than 5,000 young lives each year. That achievement would not have been possible without the health services. But neither would it have been possible without the commitment of the nation's political leaders and a society-wide alliance involving the mass media and tens of thousands of schoolteachers, religious leaders, and campaign volunteers (panel 3).

◯ *Senegal*, one of the thirty poorest nations in the world, with 30,000 vaccine-preventable deaths each year, has lifted its measles, DPT and TB immunization levels from very low levels to approximately 70% by mid-1987. Panel 2 describes the remarkable social movement which

has made that possible in a nation with low levels of literacy and mass-media coverage.

◯ *Turkey* has more than trebled its immunization coverage since 1985 in an effort which has already saved the lives of more than 20,000 Turkish children. Almost every possible organized resource in Turkish society played its part, including the mass media, over 50,000 Islamic leaders, and 200,000 schoolteachers (panel 9).

In each of these cases, dramatic achievement has been made possible by a national political leadership which has publicly committed itself to universal immunization and called upon the whole nation to participate in achieving it. "*Vaccination*," declared Senegal's President Diouf at the opening of his nation's immunization campaign, "*is everybody's business.*"

That same political commitment, that same social response, is the *sine qua non* of every successful effort to put today's health knowledge

Colombia: pupil power

5

In Colombia, the whole educational system is now being mobilized to promote the healthy development of the nation's 4 million young children.

In urban areas, 700,000 high-school pupils are being trained at school as 'health monitors'. 50,000 of them are already visiting families to advise parents on maternal and child health, and to refer mothers and children in need of care to the health services. At schools in rural areas, teachers are organizing groups of 10-to-15 parents to study ways of promoting their children's health and development. By 1990, a total of 300,000 parents will have participated in these meetings at 10,000 rural schools.

At all levels of the educational system – from primary through to university and including adult education classes – child survival and development topics are now being incorporated into the curriculum. Future generations of parents are learning, as part of their basic studies, how to promote child health.

These recent developments are all part of a national programme – called *Supervivir* – which aims to lower child mortality by one third before 1990. The programme's specific objectives are to fully immunize at least 80% of under-fives, to halve child deaths from diarrhoeal dehydration, to lower deaths from respiratory infections by at least 40%, to cut malnutrition by over 20%, and to reduce deaths from the complications of pregnancy and childbirth by more than 25%.

The programme, co-ordinated by the Ministry of Health, originated in the wake of the successful 'Immunization Crusade' of 1984. Building on the national concern aroused by that campaign, the aim is to develop a sustained movement to promote not just the survival but the normal mental and emotional development of the Colombian child. And in that cause, the programme seeks the permanent support of a wide range of organized resources, from the mass media to the education system, from government services to the voluntary agencies and community organizations.

The new force of Health Monitors is drawn from the ranks of high-school pupils (over 80% of the total), Red Cross volunteers, Scouts, the national police, kindergarten teachers, volunteers recruited by the Colombian Institute of Family Welfare, as well as from the Catholic Church. Their training is based on a special manual concentrating on six priority areas: diarrhoeal disease and oral rehydration therapy; vaccine-preventable diseases; malnutrition; acute respiratory infections; complications of pregnancy and childbirth; and the child's emotional development.

In high schools, these topics are now part of the normal curriculum. After studying the health manual in the 8th and 9th grades, pupils spend a total of 30 hours a year putting what they have learned at the disposal of poor communities.

Initially, many pupils doubted whether they would be able to perform the role expected of them, a scepticism shared by many of their teachers and some local health authorities. Parents were also worried about their children's safety when making house-to-house visits.

But so far, the programme is working well. Equipped with supplies of oral rehydration salts and leaflets on the six main child health and development topics, each pupil normally visits three families accompanied (at least on the initial visit) by a community leader. By 1990, health monitors will have visited over one million Colombian families.

Most families seem to have enjoyed and appreciated the visits. For the pupils themselves, visiting families in their homes has often been a deeply moving experience. And not the least of the benefits is that a new generation of Colombian youth is growing up with more social awareness of, and commitment to, the needs of Colombia's poor.

at the disposal of the majority. With that commitment, apparently insuperable difficulties can be and have been overcome. Every year for the last three years, the civil war in El Salvador has been stopped for three 'days of tranquillity' so that the nation's children could be immunized. And in September 1987, the city of Beirut also saw the first of three planned 'days of tranquillity' as leaders on all sides co-operated to allow the city's children to be vaccinated.

For immunization, in particular, these recent achievements show that there is no nation which cannot now meet the 1990 target no matter how far behind that nation may now appear to be. The strategy of social mobilization brings universal immunization within reach.

Oral rehydration therapy

Social mobilization is also now beginning to put the breakthrough known as oral rehydration at the disposal of many millions of parents (panel 7). And again, the importance of this breakthrough cannot be over-emphasized. Diarrhoeal dehydration is responsible for no less than one quarter of the more than 250,000 child deaths each week. Yet it can now be prevented by a therapy which is so simple that all parents can use it, so inexpensive that all families can afford it, and so effective that it is rapidly becoming a treatment of choice in the most advanced hospitals of the industrialized world.

The health services alone cannot empower a nation's parents with ORT. In most countries, the majority of doctors have themselves not been trained in its use. Retraining health professionals, at all levels, to use and to teach oral therapy, is therefore a necessary but not a sufficient condition for its promotion to a wider public. And in the countries now seriously attempting to put ORT at the disposal of all parents, it is an alliance between the health services and a wide range of new resources for health, including the schools, mass media, religious leaders, other government services, and non-governmental organizations, which is demonstrating that this *can* be done.

In *Egypt*, for example, tens of thousands of medical personnel at all levels have been trained to show parents how to use ORT and the message has been reinforced with massive television and radio coverage (fig. 12). The result, according to the chairman of the Egyptian Physicians Association, is that child deaths from diarrhoeal dehydration, which used to exceed 100,000 a year, have been "*approximately cut in half by the ORT effort*".[8]

Similarly, in *Honduras*, social marketing and mass-media efforts to promote ORT appear to have reduced diarrhoeal deaths in some areas of the country by approximately 50%. *Algeria* is also now on course for achieving its own target of making ORT available to every household before the end of 1988. *China* has a long history of using fluids for oral rehydration and ORT is now in use in the majority of China's hospitals. *Ecuador* and *Peru*, despite severe economic problems, are now making nation-wide attempts to put ORT at the disposal of every family. And in *Bangladesh*, one non-governmental organization has now organized almost 9 million home visits to teach the ORT technique to the nation's mothers (panel 8).

It is not nearly enough. Progress is far too slow. Three million children should not still be dying each year from the dehydration which any parent can prevent at a cost which any parent can afford. Yet the WHO targets to be achieved by 1989 (50% of parents using ORT, and 1.5 million children's lives being saved by it) are not going to be met unless there is a sudden acceleration of the world-wide effort to promote the ORT message over the next two years (fig. 5). Doctors and health workers need to be trained to communicate that message face to face with parents. Schools and mass media and organized religion need to be asked to reinforce it. And all political leaders not yet aware of the ORT potential need to be confronted with the fact that the main enemy of their nation's children can now be defeated, at an affordable cost, if the nation's organized resources are mobilized to meet that challenge.

Births and health

Although immunization and ORT have been the major rallying points of the alliance for

AIDS: a world-wide effort

6

The spread of AIDS over the next ten years could be reduced by 80%-90% if the public were already well informed about the disease and taking the obvious steps to avoid it. In the absence of behavioural change, the disease is likely to infect anywhere between 5 and 30 million people over the next decade.

AIDS therefore has something in common with other leading threats to human health – cancer, heart disease, diarrhoeal dehydration, respiratory infection, and malnutrition. Against all of these, the most effective weapon is education. That is why world leaders, meeting at the Venice summit in June 1987, spelt it out that "in the absence of a vaccine or a cure, the best hope for the prevention of AIDS ... rests on a strategy based on educating the public ... about the practical steps each person can take to avoid contracting or spreading it."

In the industrialized nations, billions of dollars are now being spent on information, and evidence from several cities, including London and San Francisco, indicates that the spread of AIDS is already being slowed.

In the developing world, and particularly in Africa, a massive public education effort involving not only the health services but the schools, the mass media and the voluntary agencies is also now beginning.

AIDS is therefore spurring one of the greatest health education efforts the world has ever seen. But it is precisely this kind and scale of effort which is also needed to empower parents with information against diarrhoeal disease, malnutrition, vaccine-preventable disease, and respiratory infections – the core group of health problems which are the greatest threats to the life and health of the human family, and especially of its children.

AIDS education could therefore be part of a wider effort to empower people everywhere to protect their families' health by their own actions. And if this were to happen over the next decade, then it might be that even the dark cloud of AIDS could have a silver lining of hope.

But setting AIDS in this context does not mean that AIDS itself is not a vital issue for children – particularly in Africa. Not only are many more children being orphaned by the disease in Africa than anywhere else, but more children are also contracting the disease. Unlike the industrialized world, Africa has as many women with AIDS as men. Most are in their child-bearing years and nearly half of the babies they bear also become infected. Doctors in Zambia, for example, fear that 6,000 infants may now have AIDS, fifteen times as many as the United States.

AIDS could also pose an indirect threat to millions more children if misinformation about the disease is allowed to affect immunization and breast-feeding programmes.

Theoretically, it is possible that breast-feeding can transmit the AIDS virus. World-wide there are two cases where this is thought to have happened. But the risk is minimal – whereas the abandonment of breast-feeding, in poor communities, can double and treble the risk of illness and death.

The virus can also be transmitted via unsterile needles or syringes. But the Expanded Programme on Immunization (EPI) is now reinforcing sterilization procedures world-wide and there is no known case of a child contracting the AIDS virus through an EPI injection.

Misinformation must not threaten the building of a permanent immunization system which is already saving 1.4 million children's lives each year and could save 3 million more. Nor should it be forgotten that this is a system which will benefit the whole world when a vaccine against AIDS itself is finally developed.

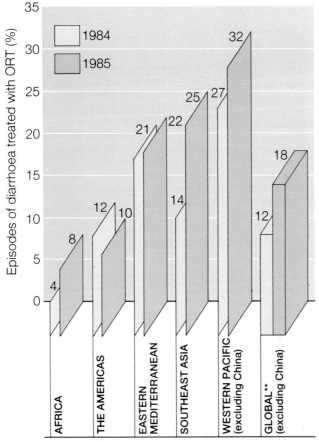

Fig. 5 Estimated ORT use rates for children under five, 1984–1985*

Episodes of diarrhoea treated with ORT (%)

1984
1985

AFRICA
THE AMERICAS
EASTERN MEDITERRANEAN
SOUTHEAST ASIA
WESTERN PACIFIC (excluding China)
GLOBAL** (excluding China)

4, 8, 12, 10, 21, 22, 25, 14, 32, 27, 12, 18

Oral rehydration therapy (ORT) can be used to prevent or correct the diarrhoeal dehydration which is the most common cause of deaths to young children. In the 1980s the promotion of sachets of oral rehydration salts (ORS), or salt and sugar solutions, or other kinds of home-made rehydration fluid, has put this therapy at the disposal of approximately 20% of the world's parents and is now saving an estimated 600,000 lives a year.

* Use rates refer to the percentage of diarrhoeal episodes in children under five years of age treated with ORT. ORT is taken here to mean oral rehydration salts (ORS), or salt and sugar solution. When estimates for both were available for a country, the midpoint between the sum and the greater of the two values was used as the ORT use rate. All numerators were calculated assuming no use of ORT in countries for which no data were available.

** When estimates of the use of ORS, salt and sugar solution, and any type of household fluid were available, and the greater of the three was used, a global minimum of 24% of episodes was estimated to have received some form of oral rehydration fluid in both 1984 and 1985.

Source:"Interim Programme Report 1986", World Health Organization, Programme for Control of Diarrhoeal Diseases, WHO/CDD/87.26.

children, there have also been other examples, in recent years, to show the power of mobilizing a wide range of social resources in the cause of child health. Throughout Latin America, for example, the battle to reach tens of millions of parents with today's information about the benefits of breast-milk and the dangers of artificial feeding has been waged through the hospitals and clinics, the television and radio stations, the newspapers and magazines, the women's movements and sports teams. Panel 11 brings together the results of such communications efforts in several nations of the developing world and panel 12 illustrates the vital role of hospital staffs in the promotion of breast-feeding.

But perhaps the greatest example in recent years of the attempt to mobilize communications capacity to empower the majority with available health knowledge and techniques, is the rapid spread of family planning across the developing world.

Planning births has usually been viewed primarily as a means of limiting population growth. But in recent years, world-wide research has shown that preventing births which come 'too many, too close, too young, too old' can do more to improve mother and child health than almost any other single intervention (fig. 10). Even if there were no such thing as a population problem, therefore, the decision of so many millions of families to begin timing the births of their children, by various methods and according to their own traditions and values, would still rank as one of this century's greatest contributions to the well-being of the human family.

In the 1960s, family planning was the province of the élite. Today, almost all adults in the developing world know about, over one half are in favour of, and over one third are using, family planning methods.

And again, this achievement is a result of a conscious decision, in country after country, to use today's new communications capacity to break family planning knowledge and techniques out from behind the walls of the clinics and begin putting them at the disposal of the public via schools and adult education classes, television and radio, newspapers and billboards, cinemas and

ORT:
a progress report

7

Two decades ago, scientists in Calcutta and Dhaka demonstrated that cholera patients could be successfully treated using a solution of glucose, salts, and water taken orally. The same treatment was soon shown to be equally effective against all forms of acute diarrhoeal dehydration – a condition which kills over 3 million young children each year. The formula soon became known as oral rehydration salts (ORS), the technique as oral rehydration therapy (ORT).

But a decade later, very few doctors in the developing world were even aware of ORT's revolutionary potential. Very few health centres had stocks of ORS available, and very few governments were even aware that anything had changed. So by the late 1970s, fewer than 1% of the developing world's children were being treated with a therapy which could have been saving some 10,000 lives a day.

In the past decade, that picture has changed:-

○ A total of 90 countries now have national programmes to promote the use of ORT.

○ Global production of ORS has reached 270 million litres a year and 47 developing countries have begun mass production of the salts (56% of world output).

○ Approximately 20% of children with diarrhoea are now being treated with either ORS or home-made oral rehydration solutions (1985 figure).

○ UNICEF now estimates that ORT may be preventing more than 600,000 deaths a year.

This global effort is being co-ordinated by WHO's Diarrhoeal Disease Control Programme which has set the ambitious target of 50% ORT use by the year 1989. If achieved, that would prevent approximately 1.5 million child deaths from diarrhoeal disease each year.

But reaching such a target will require an extraordinary effort to overcome a number of serious problems within a very short time.

Perhaps surprisingly, the most serious problem of all is the lack of doctors, nurses, and other health workers who have been properly trained in the clinical management of diarrhoea using ORT. According to WHO, only about 25% of health facilities stock ORS and only about 6% of health workers have been fully trained in its use. Even when ORT is officially recommended, most health professionals do not have any direct 'hands on' experience of the therapy and are therefore unaware of its real potential. Many doctors and health workers continue to use and to prescribe anti-diarrhoeal drugs which, in almost all cases, are either useless or harmful. And many still advise parents to withhold food from a child who has diarrhoea – the worst possible advice.

Training in diarrhoea management is neither costly nor technically difficult, but it is not one of the subjects traditionally taught to students of medicine, nursing, midwifery and other paramedical disciplines. With support from the United States Agency for International Development, WHO is now developing materials for teaching medical students about ORT. Guidelines for establishing special diarrhoea training units have already been completed. And in the 1980s, WHO has also helped to train 8,450 health professionals from 130 countries in the supervisory skills needed to implement diarrhoeal disease control programmes.

By the start of the 1990s, almost a quarter of health workers world-wide will have been trained in up-to-date methods of dealing with diarrhoeal disease, including the use of ORT. This 'critical mass' of trained personnel should ensure that ORT, combined with continued feeding, rapidly becomes the routine treatment for children with diarrhoea.

If other resources – including the schools, media, and non-governmental organizations – can also be mobilized, then it should be possible to also train all *parents* to prevent or treat diarrhoeal dehydration. And that would bring the world close to victory over the most important single cause of death and malnutrition among its young children.

stations, work-place and market-place, voluntary organizations and women's groups, as well as through the health services themselves.

The giant step

The struggle to empower all parents with the knowledge and the means to protect their children by such means as immunization, oral rehydration, timing births, and breast-feeding is therefore well under way. And the strategy of social mobilization is already showing what it can achieve on these major battlegrounds of child health.

But the involvement of large numbers of people and a wide variety of organizations in the promotion of immunization and ORT has also shown that it can be a 'thin end of the wedge' for primary health care itself. Social mobilization has shown that it can put child health onto the political agenda. It has shown that it can boost health services by giving them the lead role in a major national achievement. It has demonstrated a strategy which can now be used against other health and development problems. It has shown that it can help to create a more informed demand among communities for basic services. And it has shown that it can help people themselves to gain a little more confidence in their own ability to participate in improving their own lives.

In *Colombia*, for example, the successful immunization effort of the mid-1980s is now being followed up by a National Child Survival and Development Plan which aims to involve a wide range of resources, and especially the nation's schools, in enabling parents to reduce deaths from diarrhoeal dehydration by half and from acute respiratory infections by over one third (panel 5).

In *Egypt*, the success of the ORT programme has encouraged the nation to take on the challenge of universal immunization – and with equally remarkable results. This year, with massive television coverage and the participation of the President, the First Lady, and Islamic leaders, first-round vaccinations have reached almost 90% of the nation's infants and full immunization

was expected to reach 80% before the end of 1987.

In *Indonesia*, success in mobilizing hundreds of thousands of members of the family welfare movement as active nutrition cadres has led to the setting up of 133,000 *posyandus*, or village health posts, which now support more than half of the nation's parents in providing an integrated package of low-cost methods for protecting their children's normal health and growth.* By means of immunization, oral rehydration, family planning, the promotion of breast-feeding, pre-natal care, and monthly growth monitoring, the *posyandus* may succeed in empowering parents to reduce the 1980 child death rate by 50% or more by the end of the decade.

In *Burkina Faso*, the 1984 immunization campaign which protected 70% of the nation's under-14-year-olds against three major diseases (yellow fever, meningitis and measles) has led to the 'one village, one health post' programme which is now well on the way towards its goal of putting a community health worker in each of the nation's 7,500 villages.

In *Algeria*, an alliance between the mass media, the schools, and the health services aims to halve the nation's child death rate, so saving the lives of 40,000 Algerian children a year, by achieving universal immunization before the end of 1989 and universal knowledge of ORT before the end of 1990. Reinforcing that effort, Algeria is also rapidly approaching its goal of providing clean water nation-wide by the end of 1988.

In *Ecuador* and *Peru*, despite grave economic problems, child survival projects are now attempting, with considerable success, to support all parents in using growth promotion, ORT, immunization, and family planning as a means of drastically reducing child deaths and child malnutrition.

---

* The number of *posyandus* is scheduled to reach 200,000 by mid-1988, achieving Indonesia's target of providing one health post for every 100 children under five in the most populated areas of Indonesia, so covering 82% of all the 21 million Indonesian under-fives.

21

All of these are nation-wide efforts. In many other nations, smaller-scale projects are showing over and over again that the major causes of death, disability, and poor growth among the world's children can be effectively tackled, even at very low levels of economic development, by informing and supporting parents themselves in the use of both valid existing knowledge and the new knowledge which the world has accumulated in recent years. Every month brings new reports of pilot projects which have lowered child death rates by educating parents in oral rehydration therapy in one or other of the 90 developing countries where diarrhoeal disease control programmes have now been launched. Similarly, trials are now showing that the distribution of vitamin A capsules, or the informing of parents about the child's daily need for the vegetables which provide vitamin A, can have dramatic effects not only on preventing blindness but also on disease reduction generally. And over the last eighteen months, reports have also been coming in from many local pilot programmes which have succeeded in halving child deaths from acute respiratory infections by educating parents about the danger signs and making antibiotics available through inexpensively trained community health workers (fig. 6).

At the moment, the scale on which many of these solutions are being applied is simply not commensurate with the scale of the problems they are designed to tackle. And as Dr. Vulimiri Ramalingaswami, former Director-General of the Indian Medical Research Council, has said:-

"*We now have to make the giant step from small-scale experiments to the mass application of new techniques in a new kind of organizational framework. This process involves community participation, a village-level approach, the use of simply trained personnel indigenous to the community, together with a graded referral system, and the provision of services as an integrated package rather than in a fragmented, episodic way.*"[9]

Fig. 6 Reduction in deaths from acute respiratory infections (ARI), Thapathali, Nepal, 1984–1985

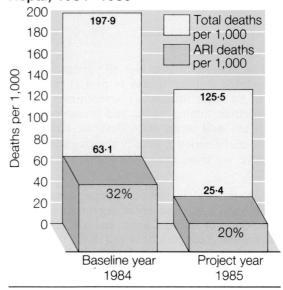

Acute respiratory infections (excluding measles) kill approximately 2 million children each year. In this project in Nepal, parents were trained to recognize the danger signs; children were immunized; health workers were trained to give antibiotics and to refer serious cases to hospital. The result, in one year, was a 60% reduction in deaths from respiratory infections.

Source: ARI news, issue 6, December 1986.

In both the scale and effectiveness of these efforts, there is still a long road to travel. But the achievements of the last few years have demonstrated beyond doubt that social mobilization, the dynamic alliance of a wide range of a society's organized resources, is now a new and powerful weapon in the struggle for human development. It is a strategy which can help in the essential development process of giving people more control over their own lives and enabling them to participate in, and to organize for, the improvement in basic living conditions which is so long overdue.

Children and recession

Despite all past failures and present frustrations, child death rates have been halved in almost every region of the developing world. Now, our generation is seeing, for the first time in human history, a fall not only in the rate but also in the absolute numbers of child deaths. In 1950, for example, the annual toll of under-five deaths exceeded 25 million. By 1980, that figure had been cut to just under 16 million. Today, it has almost certainly been brought down towards, and possibly even below, the 14 million mark.[10] And this has been achieved despite a 25% increase, since 1950, in the absolute number of births per year.

It is sometimes argued that further reductions in child deaths will exacerbate the problems of rapid population growth. But the intuitive logic of this argument does not survive closer examination. The pattern of demographic change in all nations shows that there has never been a steep and sustained fall in child births which has not been preceded by a steep and sustained fall in child deaths (panel 13). After a certain point (when the under-five mortality rate has fallen below about 100 deaths per 1,000 births) the reduction in the number of births is usually even more rapid than the reduction in child deaths. The reasons for this, and the human variables at play, are many and complex, but one constant factor is that families tend to have fewer children when they become more confident that their existing children will survive.

In addition, the new opportunities now available for further reducing child deaths can themselves help to reduce the rate of population growth in two important ways. First, key child survival strategies, such as the promotion of breast-feeding (a 'natural contraceptive') and the spacing of births at least two years apart, exert an obvious and direct downward pressure on birth rates. Second, empowering parents to protect their children's lives and growth helps to increase their sense of control over their own life and destiny, and that sense of increasing control is perhaps the one factor, above all others, which makes the acceptance of family planning more likely. Because of these many different links between reducing child deaths and reducing child births, a revolution in child survival and develop-

ment in the years ahead would in fact contribute towards the eventual stabilization of world population at an earlier date and at a lower level than would otherwise be the case.

The next advance

Such progress in reducing both child deaths and child births has been one of the greatest human achievements of this or any other century. Yet there are still an estimated 38,000 young children dying every day – yesterday, today, and tomorrow – from the combination of common infections and poor nutritional health.

What we are now seeing is the beginning of the next phase of this story, the beginning of another great health revolution which could re-accelerate progress, contribute to a continued decline in the rate of population growth, and again halve the rate of death and malnutrition among the world's young children.

The way in which this could be achieved is becoming clearer as the 1980s draw to an end. Primary health care is inching along the road from rhetoric to reality. But it is a process which can be accelerated by mobilizing today's capacity to support the vast majority of families in knowing more, doing more, and demanding more as they struggle to apply the knowledge that is now available for protecting their own and their children's health.

That strategy has already begun to be tested in the 1980s. And the results so far suggest that the child survival and development breakthrough of the late twentieth century has already begun.

The driving force behind this next advance in child well-being will not be medical or scientific. It will be political and social. For it depends upon a political commitment, at all levels of national life, to mobilize all possible organized resources behind the task of informing and supporting parents in applying today's knowledge. That is why the next chapter of this report will concentrate on what exactly that knowledge is, and on the details of the Grand Alliance which must be forged if this knowledge is to be put at the disposal of all.

Bangladesh: realities of people's lives

8

The Bangladesh Rural Advancement Committee (BRAC) is attempting to take ORT to every home in a nation where 250,000 children die every year from diarrhoeal dehydration. So far, 9 million mothers have been reached. The Director of BRAC, Fazle Hasan Abed, summarizes the lessons learned:-

After our first few months in the villages, follow-up surveys showed that only 10% of those reached were actually using ORT. So began a long process of learning about the relationship between information and behavioural change.

Our first lesson was that teachers must believe in what they are teaching. I discovered that our own workers were not using ORT themselves: they still believed more in pills and tablets. But after hospital demonstrations, they were convinced about the salt and sugar recipe. When they began to believe, those whom they taught also began to believe: and the usage rate began to rise.

We also learned that the whole community has to be prepared for new knowledge. If the men have not heard of ORT, they will discourage their wives from wasting time with it. Our male workers always meet with the men first and, with constant radio messages to back us up, ORT has become familiar to 80% of adult males in Bangladesh. They now expect their wives to know about it. Similarly, if ORT is accepted by the schoolteachers and the leading people in the community, then mothers will be more likely to use it.

To create this climate of acceptance means using every channel of communication. We even set up loudspeakers and demonstration stalls in the market-places, which are important communication centres in rural Bangladesh. We make sure all teachers train their pupils in ORT and encourage them to take health messages home.

We have also now begun to tap the potential of the mass media, using television advertising to get across nutrition messages. We know that the poor don't have television. But nowadays, the most influential people in the community do. And unless they accept new knowledge, the chances of the poor accepting it are very much reduced.

Once the community is prepared, our workers – and there are now 2,500 of them – go house to house, spending half an hour with each mother, talking about ORT and other ways of protecting children.

Above all, you have to bear in mind the realities of people's lives. If you tell people to boil water for ORT, this may mean that 50% will not use the therapy. So you have to make a pragmatic decision – should boiling water be part of the message or not?

I believe everyone should know about things like ORT and immunization, birth spacing and proper weaning. Then we will see a synergism between these improvements, leading to a fall in the dreadful death rate among our children. In this way, we can build primary health care in each mother and in each household. That is where the battle has to be won.

But communities must also demand, and governments must provide, basic health services. An informed community is more likely to do this. And an informed government bureaucracy is more likely to respond. So there is a job of advocacy to do in both directions.

Sometimes I have been discouraged. The knowledge road to health is not easy. We have reached 9 million women. Of those, about 40% have begun to use ORT. And of those, half are using it correctly. But if we look ahead fifteen years, I am certain that ORT and other vital health messages will not only be known to 100% of Bangladeshi mothers – they will also be part of our culture.

But before discussing further the possibility for another great advance for children, it must be acknowledged that both past achievement and present potential are now threatened from behind by another of the great forces affecting the daily lives of millions of people in the developing world of the 1980s.

Adjustment to recession

That threat comes from the lingering recession which still rests its crushing weight on much of the developing world and which appears unlikely to lift in the years immediately ahead as the United States, Japan, and other major industrial powers struggle with the necessary restructuring of their own economies.

With raw material prices at their lowest levels for thirty years, debt servicing claiming approximately 25% of the third world's revenues, a 60% drop in bank lending, a long period of stagnation in overseas aid, and a failure to solve international economic problems affecting both rich and poor worlds, the rate of per capita economic growth has been negative or negligible for two thirds of the developing nations in the 1980s (fig. 7).

Because several of the most populous countries of Asia, including China and India, have been able to insulate themselves from the worst of the recession, the number of people living in nations with zero or negative economic growth in the 1980s is estimated at over 700 million or just under 30% of the developing world's population (fig. 8). But three quarters of the countries in Africa and Latin America have seen their average incomes fall by 15% and 10% respectively during this decade.[11] And in Africa – from Ethiopia in the east to the Côte d'Ivoire in the west, and from the Sudan in the north to Mozambique in the south – the physical and financial droughts of recent years, combined with regional and internal conflicts, have withered a subcontinent almost to the bone.

In general, the ones who have suffered the most from this recession are the young children of poor communities in affected countries. They are the ones whose families have least scope for making economies and have therefore had to cut back on necessities. And they are the ones who are most dependent on the government services and subsidies which so many governments have felt obliged to cut back as a way of adjusting to economic recession.

It cannot be stressed too often that the young child cannot just 'ride out' such periods of austerity. Ninety per cent of the growth of a human brain and much of the growth of the human body is completed in the first five years of life. A child who has to go without adequate food or health care in those years will not grow to his or her physical or mental potential. There is no second chance.

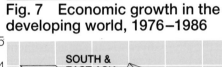

Fig. 7   Economic growth in the developing world, 1976–1986

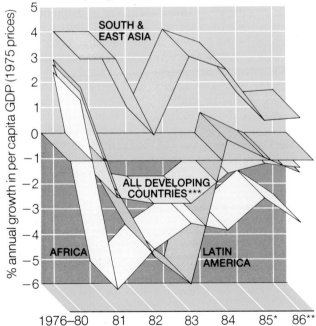

Approximately one third of the developing world's people live in countries which have experienced zero or negative economic growth in the 1980 s.

* Preliminary

** UN Secretariat forcasts

*** Market economies

Source: United Nations Department of International Economic and Social Affairs.

In the 1980s so far, more than 70 governments have had to adopt economic 'adjustment policies' in order to reduce balance-of-payments deficits, honour debt repayments, reduce inflation, and try to get their stalled economies going again. In most of those nations, such policies have involved cut-backs in government expenditure on the social services and on subsidies for staple foods.

Since 1983, UNICEF has been gleaning evidence of the impact of these processes on the well-being of the developing world's children.* The need for such a special study, and the paucity of the data available, is in itself a pointer to the lack of priority given to the protection of children in difficult economic times. But the results to date show that the well-being of the young has been measurably deteriorating in at least thirty nations of the developing world. In many African countries, for example, malnutrition is known to have increased.

Health care and education have also suffered. The number of qualified teachers lost to the education system in the early 1980s was 4,000 in Ghana and 7,000 in Zaire.

This year, in a sample of ten countries selected by UNICEF for more detailed study, malnutrition was found to have risen in five, child death rates had risen in three, and school attendance was falling in eight.

A better way

So it is that the greatest burden of recession is being passed on to the weakest and most vulnerable members of the world community.

Not even on economic grounds can such a process be justified. Sacrificing the growth of today's children for the growth of tomorrow's economy makes neither economic sense nor human sense.

Yet that is what present 'adjustment policies', with notable exceptions in some countries, have

amounted to. And what it means to millions of small children, when all the financial euphemisms of recession and adjustment are stripped away, is that the once-in-a-lifetime chance for normal growth must be forgone.

Allowing this to happen is a disgrace to the present and a threat to the future. It is the antithesis of civilization. It is a process which shames and diminishes us all.

There are practical alternatives. And the guiding principle for those alternatives is rooted in the development experience of the post-war era. For just as it was necessary to fight for 'basic needs' policies in the 1970s to try to ensure that food, health care, education and housing for the poor were given some priority in a time of economic growth, so it is now necessary to fight for a policy which protects what has been achieved and makes sure that the poor do not suffer disproportionately in a period of economic decline.

The specific alternatives to current adjustment strategies have been set out in a special UNICEF report published in 1987 under the title *Adjustment with a human face*.* At their core is the idea that the effect of adjustment policies on the most vulnerable sectors of society, and particularly its children, should be studied in advance, that such policies should seek to improve the productivity and incomes of the poor, and that subsidies and services which form part of the fabric of survival should be reinforced rather than discarded.**

---

* UNICEF's first special study on this topic, *The impact of world recession on children*, was published in 1984.

* *Adjustment with a human face*, edited by Giovanni Cornia, Richard Jolly, and Frances Stewart, is published in English in two volumes by Oxford University Press, and includes ten country case studies – Botswana, Brazil (São Paulo), Chile, Ghana, Jamaica, Peru, the Philippines, the Republic of Korea, Sri Lanka, and Zimbabwe. Volume I is also available in French as *L'Ajustement a visage humain* (Economica, Paris), and both volumes are available in Spanish as *Ajuste con rostro humano*, (Siglo XXI, Madrid).

** Most countries undertaking adjustment policies have sought financial help and stand-by credit from the International Monetary Fund (IMF). In June of 1987, IMF Managing Director Michel Camdessus told the Economic and Social Council of the United Nations in Geneva that "*Fund missions are willing – when preparing stand-by programmes, and when requested by a member country – to consider with the authorities the implications of alternative approaches to adjustment for the distribution of income, with a view in particular to sheltering the poorest.*"

To the argument that these services simply cannot be afforded, the answer must be that this is again a question not of inevitabilities but of priorities. Even if a government has to make steep spending cuts, there is a choice to be made about exactly where those cuts should be made. In defence or in the health of its people? In subsidies to national airlines serving the richest 2% or to national food programmes serving the poorest 20%? And even if spending on health and education does have to take its share of the financial strain, there still remains a choice about whether to cut into the budgets of universities or primary schools, city hospitals or rural primary health care clinics, cardiac research or child immunization programmes.

It is at this point that the whole issue of adjustment to economic recession joins hands with the main theme of this report. For 'adjustment with a human face' does not just mean that economic constraints can be disregarded. It means, rather, that the maximum protection for the most vulnerable has to be squeezed from every dollar available for health care, education, or social welfare. And there is no question at all that the major opportunities for achieving that aim now lie in mobilizing existing capacity to inform and support parents in applying today's knowledge about such basic health actions as immunization, oral rehydration therapy, birth spacing, breast-feeding, safe weaning, growth monitoring, control of respiratory infections, safe motherhood, and basic hygiene.

These are the major battlegrounds of child health. These are the areas of action which could cut child deaths and child malnutrition by half. These are the areas where present knowledge could empower parents themselves to protect the lives and growth of their children. These are the areas where action is possible at such low cost that it can be afforded by almost any nation and by almost any family even in such difficult economic times.

To mobilize a society's existing resources in order to inform and support parents in this way is the key to 'adjustment with a human face'. It makes it possible to protect the vulnerable, even under economic pressure. It demonstrates a practical concern for the well-being of the majority and not just the élite. It is therefore not only more civilized and more humane. It also makes more economic and political sense.

Some countries are attempting to pioneer this response to recession. *Indonesia*, for example, faced with the need to cut overall spending as a result of falling oil revenues, has cut back its hospital investment costs by 75%. At the same time, funding has actually been increased to accelerate the development of the *posyandus* (200,000 of them by March 1988) which are providing immunization and family planning

Fig. 8 Percentage of the developing world's population living in countries with zero or negative growth in per capita GDP, 1979–1985

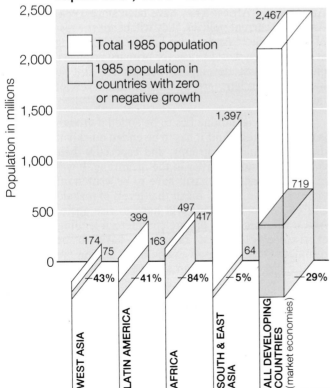

With the recession of the 1980s, average living standards have fallen in countries which are home to 29% of the developing world's people.

Source: United Nations Division of Economic and Social Affairs.

services, and assisting parents with oral rehydration therapy and growth monitoring, in over 47,000 villages. *India* is also restraining expenditure on hospitals while stepping up programmes to provide immunization and other vital low-cost services to the majority. *Chile* has increased its spending on social services targeted to the poorest even though overall government expenditures have been cut back. And in *Algeria*, where spending cuts have been made this year in every ministry except the Ministry of Health, hospital spending has also been held back while the nation attempts to put oral rehydration therapy, immunization, and clean water at the disposal of every family in the nation.

The international responsibility

But as the new UNICEF report points out, *"for some countries, national action alone cannot be sufficient, even with the most heroic political and economic efforts"*.[12] If long-term economic growth is to be restored, and if the most vulnerable members of society are to be protected in the process, then the industrialized world will have to offer fairer aid and trade policies and further financial help. Without it, 'adjustment with a human face' will be a slogan which will never be reflected on the face of a child.

In many nations today, children are going without food or health care or schooling because of a financial drought which cannot easily be captured by television cameras. Yet the lack of financial resources can be just as harrowing as lack of rainfall for those who are its victims. In Brazil alone, for example, an estimated 60,000 children have died as a result of recession in the 1980s.[13]

This crisis is not only of the poor world's making. Despite all past mistakes in policy or priority, the fact is that many of the elements in the economic storm – falling commodity prices, high interest rates, an unstable dollar, fluctuating oil prices, falling aid levels – have been beyond the influence of those who have been hardest hit.

Such a dramatic deterioration in the economic climate for the developing world in the 1980s is not widely appreciated in the industrialized nations, perhaps because its causes cannot be so readily understood or its consequences so easily photographed as the deterioration in the physical climate which has become part of our standard imagery of the developing world in this decade. But the change from the 70s to the 80s has been such that the net flow of financial resources between rich and poor worlds has been almost completely reversed in the last five years. Figure 9 shows that when all the calculations are done, taking into account aid and loans, interest and amortization payments, investments and returns, the bottom line is that the developing world transferred over $30 billion to the industrialized world in 1985. That is a dramatic about-face. In 1980, the net transfer was over $40 billion from the rich to the poor. Even the World Bank and the International Monetary Fund themselves are now net recipients of resources from Latin America and Africa. They have been since 1984. And, with current policies, they will be for the rest of this decade.[14] And all this has been happening at a time when world prices for primary products, on which most developing nations are still so heavily dependent, are at their lowest levels of modern times.

This financial famine has to be ended if growth is to be restored. And it has to be ended quickly if the most vulnerable groups, and especially their children, are not to suffer in the meantime. It will mean that many debts will have to be written off or restructured. It will mean that levels of real aid and concessionary loans will have to rise again. And it will mean that private commercial lending at reasonable interest rates will have to be resumed. Only increased co-operation among the industrialized countries can achieve this.

In the slightly longer term, the restoration of economic growth to large areas of the developing world will depend, most of all, on an expanding world economy accompanied by a reduction in interest rates, a range of commodity agreements to secure fair and stable prices for raw materials, and a rolling back of the protectionism which is gradually stifling the third world's ability to sell to, and buy from, the industrialized world. Difficult as these measures might be to agree on and co-ordinate, they are in the long-term politi-

Fig. 9 Decline in net transfer of resources to the capital-importing developing countries, 1980–1985

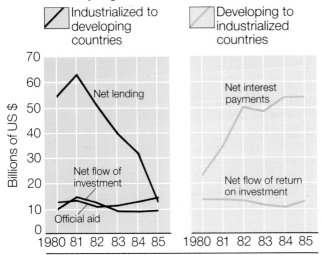

Net transfer of resources between industrialized and developing worlds

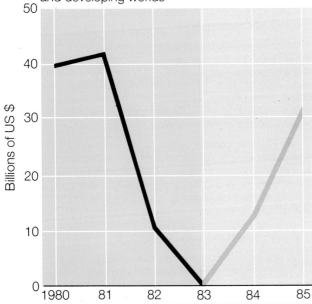

Taking into account investment, official aid, and private lending, and subtracting repayments of interest and capital, the net flow of resources is now from the developing world to the industrialized world.

Source: United Nations Department of International Economic and Social Affairs, 1986.

cal and economic interests of all nations, the only sure foundation for sustained prosperity, stability, and peace.

As a practical beginning for this process, any government which now demonstrates a willingness to put the poor first, to use its power as a shock absorber for the most vulnerable on the rough road of recession, should now have the generous support of the industrialized world. For as the Director of Oxfam UK has said: "*Eight hundred million people who spend part of each year malnourished need help today, not in a future age when – after fifteen years of economic growth – their governments are better placed for responding to the needs of the poor.*"

But for the industrialized world to play its part, those who feed and shape public opinion also have a difficult and urgent job to do. Somehow, a new ethos has to be created, a new ethos which sees the 'silent emergency' of frequent infection and widespread malnutrition as being just as unacceptable as the loud emergency of sudden starvation. The former Administrator of the United Nations Development Programme, Bradford Morse, has called for that new ethos in these words:-

"*When once they had been fully informed, the peoples said 'No!' to the spectre of catastrophe spreading among 35 million of their extended family in Africa. If the peoples of the United Nations are mobilized to say 'No!' to the perennial poverty in which 800 million of the human family live, and demand the full mobilization of their governments and of the United Nations system and other multilateral instrumentalities to attack it, then it can be done.*"[15]

Finally, if the principle of protecting the most vulnerable is to be taken seriously, then it must be a process which can be monitored and measured. And the fact is that whereas most nations can and do produce up-to-date quarterly statistics on the health of their economies, few nations can produce even annual statistics on the health of their children. This failure to monitor the effects of economic and social changes on the well-being of the most vulnerable, and particularly on the growing minds and bodies of young children, is both a cause and a symptom of the lack of political

Turkey: sustaining an achievement

9

In late 1985, Turkey mounted one of the most impressive immunization campaigns ever seen. Over 4 million children were vaccinated and coverage rose to over 80% for the main vaccine-preventable diseases. As a result, over 3 million cases of measles, whooping cough, and polio – and an estimated 22,000 child deaths – were prevented.

All this was made possible by social mobilization on a grand scale – bringing together the health services, the mass media, over 200,000 teachers, more than 50,000 imams, and thousands of volunteers from the Rotary Clubs, the Red Crescent, the women's groups, and the Lions Clubs.

But since that time, 3 million new babies have been born in Turkey. And over 1.5 million more will be born in 1988. Are they too being immunized? And is any progress being made towards more comprehensive primary health care?

In the months following the campaign, the news was disquieting. The health services, and all who had helped in the great achievement, rested or turned their attention to other urgent tasks. Snow made many villages inaccessible. Holidays, cancelled during the campaign, were taken. And the different government ministries, which had worked together so successfully, began to go back to their own turf. Meanwhile, children continued to be born… and immunization coverage began to fall.

The Ministry of Health knew that what had been won was a battle, not a war. The campaign had cleared the large backlog of unimmunized children and united Turkey in an achievement which had become a matter of national pride. The harder task of sustaining that achievement still remained.

But the campaign had also set child health high on the nation's agenda. And the establishment of a permanent service to immunize all children in their first year of life has become such an established goal that it will be a national disappointment if it is not achieved by 1990. The country, its leaders, and its health system, are committed to that target. And that commitment is what has made

new action possible during the last twelve months:-

O The President has televised an appeal to the nation, calling on all parents to immunize their children and urging all organizations to help.

O All 67 provincial governors have been notified that immunization coverage is expected to return to 80% in every province by 1988.

O All 67 provincial health directors have met with their counterparts in education, for the first time, to enlist the permanent support of 250,000 primary-school teachers in promoting immunization and other health messages.

O Television and radio promotion of immunization has continued, and expanded into other child health messages, with the support of leading figures from the entertainment world.

O New immunization rounds have been held in rural and poorer urban areas.

The result is that immunization coverage, now a high priority in the permanent national health programme, has risen again to 75% for DPT and polio, and to 50% for measles (August 1987 figures). New policies, including permanent immunization facilities at all out-patient clinics, will help to sustain those impressive levels.

Turkey's new commitment has also catalysed other primary health care action. All hospitals now use oral rehydration therapy as standard practice. The rectors of all 22 medical faculties and the heads of paediatric departments are strengthening child survival strategies in all medical and nursing curricula. Retraining programmes are being set up for all practising doctors and nurses.

The energy and commitment unleashed in late 1985 is therefore helping to pave the way towards more permanent and comprehensive primary health care for Turkish children. But the achievement of a universal and sustainable immunization programme by 1990 still stands as both the symbol and the test of that commitment.

priority afforded to this task. Yet there could be no more important test for any government than the test of whether or not it is protecting the nation's vulnerable and whether or not it is protecting the nation's future – and its children are both.

Today, the indicators for measuring the performance of that duty – the quarterly measurement of, for example, changes in child nutrition, immunization coverage, and the prevalence of low birth-weights – are not even in place. Indeed we know far more about changes in the weather or in viewing figures for television shows, or in consumer preferences and the monthly sales of video recorders, than we do about changes in the nutritional health of the under-fives.

UNICEF, WHO, and the Food and Agriculture Organization of the United Nations (FAO) are now co-operating to find ways and means of more sensitively monitoring the nutritional health of a nation's children so that, as with national economic indicators, up-to-date quarterly figures can be produced for politicians, press, and public.

Progress as measured by such indicators should become both an aim and a measure of development policy. In times of economic growth, they could reveal whether or not the poorest groups were sharing equally in the benefits of that growth. In leaner years, they would reveal whether the poor and the vulnerable were suffering disproportionately from the effects of recession and adjustment policy. They would also serve as a guide to the fulfilment of the present potential for significant low-cost progress in protecting the lives and the normal growth of the developing world's children.

And it is to the question of how that potential might be realized that this report now returns.

Family knowledge

The potential for making rapid progress in reducing child deaths and child malnutrition, even against the uphill gradient of recession, arises at this time because there is now a greater gap than ever before in history between what has been discovered and what is being applied, between what is known to health professionals and what is being made known to parents, between what could be done and what is being done.

Today, in all nations, organized social resources have reached the level of development at which it is possible to inform and support the great majority of families in taking advantage of today's knowledge. But that new capacity has to be consciously mobilized.

So far, the most significant examples of social mobilization for development objectives have been the spread of family planning and the spread of the 'green revolution'. In both cases, many millions of families have been empowered to improve their own lives through the dissemination of available knowledge and affordable technologies.

That same strategy is now beginning to be used to put two of the most powerful of all public health technologies, immunization and ORT, at the disposal of a significant percentage of the world's parents.

But as yet, the surface of this 'social mobilization' potential has hardly been scratched. And the effort to use today's communications capacity to empower people with today's knowledge cannot be limited to short-term campaigns.

Social mobilization could also be used to empower people with the knowledge to improve other basic dimensions of their lives. It could bring improvements in housing and water supply,

India: the threshold of immunity

10

A mid-course review of India's immunization effort, the largest anywhere, suggests a cautious optimism. A great surge is undoubtedly underway towards the goal of immunizing all infants and pregnant women by 1990. But there is equally no doubt that only the most rigorous local planning and programme management can raise immunization levels in the regions which still lag behind.

The stakes are high. In the early 1980s, vaccine-preventable diseases were estimated to be claiming the lives of 1 million children annually.

Results are reinforcing the strategy adopted in 1985 when the Prime Minister committed the nation to universal immunization as a 'living memorial' to the memory of the late Indira Gandhi. An Expanded Programme of Immunization was already in operation in all of India's 420 districts. Within that structure, the plan was to work district by district to 'deepen' immunization coverage from an average of below 30% to 80% or more.

In 1986, this plan went into action in 92 of the 420 districts. The coverage achieved so far is 63% for TB and polio, 68% for DPT, and 40% for measles. These figures compare with a national average of 33% for TB, 30% for polio, 35% for DPT, and 9% for measles.

In other words, coverage has been roughly doubled (and for measles quadrupled) in these 92 districts, with almost a quarter of India's population, which have been tackled to date.

In 1987, the programme has moved into another 90 districts to reach a total of 10 million infants and 11 million pregnant women. Maintaining the new level of immunization in the original 92 districts, while extending it to 90 more, is an enormous undertaking involving the coaxing of a vast and complicated system into co-ordinated action across a subcontinent diverse in language and culture, climate and terrain.

Overall, the achievement on the supply side of the immunization equation – vaccine production, refrigerated distribution, and the training of health workers, administrators and engineers – has to be judged as remarkable. In 1986, for example, 4,800 doctors, 72,000 paramedics, and 30,000 other community workers were trained to help in the effort. Secretaries of all state health departments and key people in each state administration are now being trained every year in immunization.

But reaching and sustaining a nation-wide immunization coverage of 80% or more will depend just as much on creating the demand as on ensuring the supply. And it is the demand side which still lags behind.

In every district, the plan is to mobilize all possible communications resources to raise public knowledge of, and demand for, the full vaccination of all infants. Members of parliament and religious leaders, associations of health professionals and businessmen, *panchayat* members and community elders, schoolteachers and child care workers, sports personalities and the folk media, women's groups and youth organizations, are all now beginning to support the health services in promoting the immunization message. So far, for example, 500,000 Indian primary-school teachers have been oriented on infant immunization and printed materials have been distributed widely through primary schools.

Radio and television are reaching tens of millions with the immunization message. And an estimated 100 million people are seeing advertisements for immunization in over 12,700 cinemas.

In other words, the capacity for information and support which India has built up in recent years is now being mobilized to achieve a great social objective – the saving of a million children's lives each year by universal immunization. If that goal can be achieved and sustained, then the immunization effort of the late 1980s may also have pioneered a path for progress against the many other major problems of health and nutrition which still confront the nation's children.

food security and education, economic productivity and income-earning opportunities. As important as any of these, it could promote today's knowledge and low-cost technologies for lightening the work-load of women.* In all of these areas, new and vital knowledge is now available. And in all of these areas, that knowledge could be put at the disposal of the majority by mobilizing already existing communications resources.

But it is on the plane of child health that the greatest of all gains could now be made. Today, a solid scientific consensus stands behind a body of knowledge, traditional as well as modern, discovered or rediscovered,** which could enable most families to prevent and treat almost all of the major causes of child death and child malnutrition by methods which they can understand and at a cost which they can afford.

Putting that body of information at the disposal of all families is a task as enormous as the rewards it offers. It is the great health challenge of our times. And to meet that challenge, it will be necessary to forge a new public health alliance, to stimulate a new and *permanent mobilization* of a wide range of conventional and unconventional resources in the cause of health.

For as the WHO's Director-General, Dr. Halfdan Mahler, has said:-

"Too many of us still think in terms of medical care systems or interventions rather than thinking along new lines in order to understand the determinants of the new problems and to grasp opportunities that reach far beyond the health care system... We do not need just a little bit more health education here and a little bit more health education there; we need a new approach to public health action and we need a strong public health alliance to move us forward."[16]

But in order to appreciate the nature of that alliance, and the practical tasks it would face, it is perhaps useful to briefly summarize the information it could convey.*

That knowledge is not complicated and should never be allowed to be made so. And what follows is a simple summary of a scientific consensus, a brief pulling together of a body of knowledge which should now belong not only to the medical profession but to all families everywhere:-

○ WHAT FAMILIES HAVE A RIGHT TO KNOW ABOUT TIMING BIRTHS

The health risks to both mothers and children are seriously increased by becoming pregnant before the age of 18, becoming pregnant before the last-born child is two years old, and becoming pregnant after having four children or after reaching the age of 35.

WHY FAMILIES HAVE A RIGHT TO KNOW

Because research in many nations has now shown that deaths of infants and mothers could be reduced by an estimated 25% through avoiding births which are 'too many or too close' (fig. 10) and to mothers who are 'too young or too old'.[17]

○ WHAT FAMILIES HAVE A RIGHT TO KNOW ABOUT PREGNANCY

In pregnancy, it is essential to get more food and rest each day; to register for pre-natal care if at all possible; to be immunized against tetanus; to know when something is going wrong with the pregnancy; and to arrange for a trained person to attend the birth.

---

* A review of low-cost technologies which are specifically designed to help women to save time and energy in food production, and also increase their skills and incomes, has recently been published by the International Women's Tribune Centre, 777 United Nations Plaza, New York, NY 10017, USA.

** Some traditional treatments for diarrhoea, such as carrot soups and rice conjees, have been found to be effective solutions for preventing dehydration. Similarly, certain traditional methods of preparing weaning foods, such as the use of flour made from sprouted grains, are also known to increase the energy density of a given amount of gruel or porridge – a vital factor in meeting the nutritional needs of the young child.

* Under the title *Facts for Life*, UNICEF and WHO are now bringing that knowledge together in simple and accessible form under the major headings of 'what every family has a right to know' about:-

Timing births	Safe motherhood
Breast-feeding	Promoting child growth
Immunization	Diarrhoea
Respiratory infections	Home hygiene
Malaria	AIDS

WHY FAMILIES HAVE A RIGHT TO KNOW

Each year, an estimated 500,000 mothers die in pregnancy or childbirth (leaving behind over 1 million motherless children) and over 5 million infants are stillborn or die within the first week of life.[18] Many of those deaths could now be prevented if parents, including fathers, were empowered with today's knowledge about safe pregnancy and childbirth.* Tetanus, for example, kills approximately 1 million new-borns each year, yet all of those deaths could be prevented by immunization of the mother-to-be.

As World Bank President Barber Conable said at the recent (1987) Safe Motherhood Conference in Nairobi: "*Common decency tells us that it is intolerable that 1,400 women die every day in the process of carrying or delivering their children. And common sense tells us that these needless deaths waste not only precious lives but precious human resources.*"

○ WHAT FAMILIES HAVE A RIGHT TO KNOW ABOUT BREAST-FEEDING

Bottle-feeding in the first few months of an infant's life is dangerous in poor communities. The best protection against both infection and undernutrition is exclusive breast-feeding from birth to the age of four to six months. Other foods should then be added, but breast-milk is the best food a child will ever have and breast-feeding should continue well into the second year of life.

WHY FAMILIES HAVE A RIGHT TO KNOW

In poor communities, rates of infection and death are commonly two to three times higher for bottle-fed infants than for infants who are exclusively breast-fed for the first few months of life.[19] In particular, diarrhoea is both more common and more dangerous when infants in poor com-

munities are bottle-fed. Halting the trend to artificial feeding can therefore save tens of thousands of children's lives.

○ WHAT FAMILIES HAVE A RIGHT TO KNOW ABOUT PROMOTING GROWTH

About half-way through the child's first year of life, other foods are needed in addition to breast-milk if the infant is not to become malnourished. Keeping a young child growing well from this time on, when infection and malnutrition are most dangerous and most likely, is one of the most important skills of parenthood and should involve both mother and father.

The basics are that a child needs to be fed twice as often as an adult, and that gruels or porridges should be enriched with small amounts of whatever oils or fats are available. And at all times, a child's food and drink should be kept clean.

Regular weight gain is the best single indicator of a child's normal, healthy development. If a child does not put on weight over any two-month period, something is wrong and help should be sought from a health worker or clinic.

When recovering from an illness, especially diarrhoea or measles, a small child needs an extra meal each day for every day the illness lasted. A child has not fully recovered until he or she catches up on any weight-gain lost during the illness itself.

WHY FAMILIES HAVE A RIGHT TO KNOW

Undernutrition is a factor in approximately one third of all today's child deaths. Its main cause is the combination of frequent infection and a failure to inform parents about the special feeding needs of the young child (see page 3 and footnote). With basic knowledge and support, the malnutrition and poor mental and physical growth of many millions of children could be prevented by parents themselves. In most cases, lack of information and too many demands on the mother's time and energy are a greater difficulty than the lack of food.

○ WHAT FAMILIES HAVE A RIGHT TO KNOW ABOUT IMMUNIZATION

All pregnant women should be immunized against tetanus and all children should be taken for a full

---

* "*The question we must ask is why this happens: is it because the majority of these women are poor that they are allowed to suffer this silent carnage? ... We need to generate the political commitment to reallocate resources to implement the available strategies that can reduce maternal mortality by an estimated 50% in one decade.*" Halfdan Mahler, Director-General, World Health Organization, "The safe motherhood initiative: a call to action", *The Lancet*, March 1987.

course *of immunizations before the age of one year. This will mean at least four separate vaccination visits.*

WHY FAMILIES HAVE A RIGHT TO KNOW

Approximately 800,000 infants die each year of neonatal tetanus, which can be prevented by immunizing the mother-to-be.

Approximately 300,000 children die each year of whooping cough because they did not receive a full course of DPT injections. On average, even when vaccination is available, one third of all children are not brought for the first injection and, of those who are brought, one quarter do not complete the course.[20]

Approximately 2 million children die each year because they are not immunized against measles. Only one low-cost injection is needed, but it is vital that parents bring their children as soon as possible after the age of nine months.*

○ WHAT FAMILIES HAVE A RIGHT TO KNOW ABOUT DIARRHOEA

Diarrhoea is dangerous. It is the most common disease of childhood. But it is also the most common cause of malnutrition and death. The danger to the child's life comes from the emptying of too much fluid from the body. When a child has diarrhoea, it is therefore essential to keep on giving food and fluids. Advice to 'rest the bowel' is exactly the wrong advice and should be ignored – even if it comes from a doctor. If the diarrhoea lasts more than three days, or seems much worse than usual, or if the child will not eat or drink and vomits frequently, then it is essential to seek help from a clinic, health worker, or doctor. But in the great majority of cases, all necessary action is within the power of the well-informed parent.

If the diarrhoea is not to cause malnutrition, then an extra meal a day is needed for at least a week after the illness is over.

WHY FAMILIES HAVE A RIGHT TO KNOW

Dehydration caused by diarrhoea kills 3 million children a year. And even though the chances of death in any one case of childhood diarrhoea are very small, the possibility must be protected against.[21]

For the 90% of children for whom the disease does not become life-threatening, the danger is malnutrition. If diarrhoea comes four or five or

---

Fig. 10   Infant deaths by birth interval, selected surveys

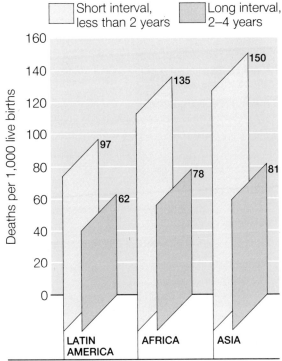

Infant deaths rise steeply when the space between births is less than two years.

Source: ''Birth Spacing Prevents Child Deaths'', Center for Population and Family Health, Columbia University, 1986.

---

* The critical factor in measles immunization is timing; immunization before the age of nine months runs the risk of the vaccine being rendered ineffective by the natural antibodies acquired through the mother. Immunizing later than nine months means that a significant proportion of children will contract measles in the interval between the wearing off of natural protection and the introduction of the vaccine. The most effective compromise is immunization as close to the age of nine months as possible. In industrialized nations, where higher levels of nutrition, housing, and immunization, mean that measles is less common and less severe, the recommended age for immunization is 12 to 15 months.

Breast-feeding: a progress report

11

For all babies, breast-milk is better than bottle-feeding. It is more nutritious, more hygienic, cheaper, and 'immunizes' infants against common infections. But the poorer the family, the greater the danger of bottle-feeding. Mixing milk-powder with unclean water in an unsterile bottle means more illnesses, more malnutrition, and a higher death rate.

The trend towards bottle-feeding in the developing world therefore puts at risk the lives and growth of many millions of infants. That is why the 1981 World Health Assembly, representing over 150 governments, adopted the International Code of Marketing of Breast-milk Substitutes to try to stop the irresponsible promotion of infant formulas and encourage the promotion of information about the advantages of breast-milk.

So far, over 130 nations have taken some action on the Code, either enforcing it by law or adopting it as a voluntary measure. But it is still too early to say whether the battle is being won or lost:-

In Latin America, seven nations have adopted the Code as law and most have launched public education campaigns. In state maternity hospitals, rooming-in of new-born babies with their mothers is becoming standard practice and mothers are being encouraged to breast-feed from birth. As a result, the trend towards bottle-feeding may have been reversed. This year, **Uruguay** became the first Latin American country to report a nation-wide increase in both the prevalence and duration of breast-feeding. Surveys are also showing local increases in **Brazil**, **Panama**, **Costa Rica**, and **Chile**.

In the **Philippines**, the trend may also have been reversed as a result of a nation-wide advertising campaign, backed up by a tough new legal code on the promotion of infant formulas, and the introduction of rooming-in at most state hospitals. In **China**, urban hospitals are now introducing rooming-in after finding out that only 20% of mothers were still breast-feeding their babies at four months (compared to 90% in rural areas).

In Africa, breast-feeding until well into the second year of a child's life is still almost universal in rural areas. But breast-feeding needs protection in the rapidly expanding urban areas.

A major problem for the years ahead can already be seen in countries such as **Brazil** and **Mexico**, where two thirds of all women of child-bearing age go out to work. Many of them find bottle-feeding more convenient, especially as it means that infants can be fed by other members of the family. So without government legislation – and employer compliance – on such issues as maternity leave and breast-feeding facilities, educational efforts can only go so far.

The struggle needs support from all sides:-

Hospitals can:-

○ keep mothers and babies together in maternity wards and encourage breast-feeding from birth

○ refuse free infant formula and ban feeding-bottles from the wards

○ teach the importance and the technique of breast-feeding to all nurses and medical students

Doctors and health workers can:-

○ explain the benefits of breast-feeding to all mothers and learn to help with any problems

The media can:-

○ inform all parents about the importance of breast-feeding

○ refuse advertising for breast-milk substitutes

○ report local violations of the infant formula code

Schools can:-

○ make sure that no child leaves school without knowing the importance of breast-feeding

Mothers who have breast-fed can:-

○ advise and encourage younger mothers in their families and neighbourhoods.

six times a year – taking away the appetite, limiting the absorption of food, burning up calories in fever, draining away nutrients – then the slow advance of malnutrition is usually the result. Diarrhoeal disease is probably responsible for up to half of all child undernutrition.[22] Plenty of fluids during the illness, and extra food in the recovery period, are the best protection.

○ WHAT FAMILIES HAVE A RIGHT TO KNOW ABOUT ACUTE RESPIRATORY INFECTIONS

A child with a bad cough or cold should be kept warm and well-fed and given plenty to drink. Breast-feeding should continue. If the child with a cough will not drink, or begins breathing much faster than normal, then the child is in danger and every effort should be made to get help quickly from a clinic or health worker.

WHY FAMILIES HAVE A RIGHT TO KNOW

Coughs and colds, along with diarrhoeal disease, are childhood's most common ailment. Most children recover on their own. But acute respiratory infections kill 2 to 3 million children a year. If the danger signs are recognized in time, the majority of parents could get help from a health worker or clinic. And most of those children could be saved by inexpensive antibiotics.

It is now known that 'fast breathing' (breathing more than 50 times a minute) is as reliable a guide to the presence of moderate and severe lung infection as the most sophisticated diagnosis available from the most qualified paediatrician in the most modern hospital. All parents could now be empowered with that knowledge.[23]

If the medical establishment would also empower community health workers to prescribe antibiotics, then another major cause of child deaths could now be drastically reduced.

○ WHAT FAMILIES HAVE A RIGHT TO KNOW ABOUT HOME HYGIENE

Many childhood illnesses, and especially diarrhoea, are caused by germs entering the mouth. If at all possible, latrines should be used or faeces disposed of so that they cannot come into contact with people, food, or drinking water. Water from unclean sources should be boiled and cooled before drinking. Hands should always be washed after defecation and before preparing or eating food. Food and water should be kept clean.

WHY FAMILIES HAVE A RIGHT TO KNOW

Many childhood illnesses, and therefore much childhood malnutrition, could be prevented by home hygiene. Lack of basic services such as clean water and safe sanitation means that home hygiene is difficult to put into practice in poor and under-served communities. But this does not mean that parents do not have a right to know why their children fall ill so often and what needs to be done – by their government, by their community, and by their own efforts – to prevent it. An informed community is also more likely to demand, and to participate in, the provision of the basic community services which make home hygiene possible.

Smoking, alcohol and AIDS

Finally, all families in both industrialized and developing nations have a right to today's facts about AIDS, and about the health risks of tobacco smoking and alcohol abuse.

It may be thought that these are chiefly adult concerns lying beyond the mandate of UNICEF. But their profound effects on children are now a daily reality in most nations.

Tobacco smoking affects children by polluting their environment and exposing them to higher-than-necessary risks of both respiratory infections and cancer. In particular, alcohol and tobacco can affect the unborn child and increase the risk of low birth-weight. So well-established are these risks that Finland has now made it illegal to smoke tobacco in the presence of a woman who is pregnant. Similarly, alcohol abuse is also closely associated with accidents, violence, neglect, and increasing poverty – events and processes to which young children are always the most exposed. Indirectly, both smoking and alcohol abuse often mean that family resources are diverted at the expense of meeting the basic needs of children.

Honduras: teaching hospitals

12

In 1982, leading hospitals in Honduras, as in many other nations today, were routinely separating mothers and babies into different wards at birth, distributing commercial infant formula to all new mothers, and bottle-feeding new-born babies with glucose and water in the first few days of life.

Most doctors and nurses were not recommending breast-feeding to mothers and very few were able to offer any advice on the subject. So although most women started breast-feeding, infant formulas were usually introduced during the first month. On average, breast-feeding had stopped altogether by the time a baby was five months old.

By 1982, up-to-date health professionals were becoming concerned about the effects of infant formulas and early weaning. By that time, it was known that exclusive breast-feeding from birth to at least the age of four months is the best guarantee of nutritional health for any child. But breast-feeding was not being supported in the hospitals where most of the nation's children were being born.

In September 1982, the PROALMA project (Proyecto de Apoyo a la Lactancia Materna) was started in three of the nation's hospitals with the aim of changing standard practices in maternity wards and retraining all doctors and nurses in the advantages of breast-feeding. Rooming-in of new-born babies with their mothers became routine. Mothers were encouraged to begin breast-feeding as soon as possible. Infant formula, feeding-bottles, and sugar and water solutions, were stopped.

By 1985, the number of health professionals recommending breast-feeding from birth had risen from 40% to 75%. The proportion of nurses recommending breast-feeding on demand rose from 33% to 90%.

As a result, the proportion of mothers helped to begin breast-feeding in the maternity ward rose from 10% in 1982 to 70% in 1985. The use of infant formula in the first month of life was almost halved. And the average length of breast-feeding rose from five months to over one year.

These changes are protecting the lives and the normal growth of babies in the cities of Tegucigalpa and San Pedro Sula at little or no cost to the health services (one of the hospitals is already saving $14,500 a year on infant formula, feeding-bottles, and glucose solution). With the help of the United States Agency for International Development, the PROALMA project is now expanding to cover all maternity wards in Honduras.

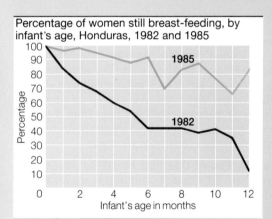

Percentage of women still breast-feeding, by infant's age, Honduras, 1982 and 1985

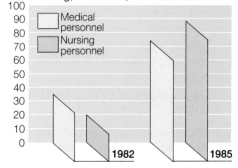

Percentage of health professionals recommending breast-feeding, Honduras, 1982 and 1985.

Source: "Breastfeeding Promotion in Honduras", Mothers and Children, vol. 6, no. 1, American Public Health Association, 1987.

These problems will not simply vanish in the daylight of health information. They are related to some of the most ingrained social and economic evils of our times. Often, for example, smoking and alcohol abuse are most common among the poor, not because the poor love their children less or are weaker-willed, but because it is among the poor that the understandable need for escapism is greater, because it is among the poor that the problems of unemployment and demoralization are most acute, because it is among the poor that self-image and self-respect are threatened every day by a consumer society from which they are, by definition, marginalized.

The deep-rootedness of such problems is a fundamental, social, economic and political challenge. But the empowering of all families with the basic facts on the health risks of tobacco, smoking and alcohol abuse has already proved that it has a major part to play in reducing the risks to society – and its children. The tobacco industry is increasingly targeting poor and minority groups in particular and the developing world in general – for it is in these sectors that room for expansion is perceived. It is therefore especially important that all responsible channels of communication are mobilized to ensure that every family is aware of the risks of tobacco smoking and alcohol abuse.

The new threat of AIDS is also beginning to have a major impact on children in two principal ways. First, many young children are being orphaned by AIDS because of the age-range of its victims. Second, increasing numbers of infants are now being infected before or during birth. This problem is particularly acute and tragic in Africa where, unlike most regions of the world, the AIDS virus appears to be striking at men and women in equal numbers. As a result, there are now (1987) estimated to be over 6,000 infants with AIDS in Zambia alone (as opposed to approximately 400 in the United States). On the horizon is an additional worry – the rising cost of the AIDS pandemic which may threaten essential services for children. In 1987, public education is the best defence we have against the AIDS threat. And information about safer sex must now be added to the lexicon of what every family should know about the protection of family health.

Partners in the alliance

This core of basic information addresses major child health problems in almost all nations. It is information on which almost all scientists are now agreed. It is information on which all parents could now act. It is therefore information which all families now have a right to know.

The first step in putting that information at the disposal of the majority is the 'tailoring' of such messages to national needs.

Centres of medical expertise in each country need to become involved in customizing, without complicating, this basic information. For although the knowledge just outlined is universally relevant, the priority of problems varies from region to region. Information about the advantages of breast-feeding and the dangers of bottle-feeding, for example, is more relevant to urban Latin America than to rural Africa. In some mountainous or flood-prone regions, a lack of iodine in the diet causes mental and physical retardation among a significant proportion of children; if parents in those regions were fully informed about this problem then they would be more likely to use and to demand iodized salt.

Similarly, the nature of the social alliance needed to promote health information, and the communications techniques employed, will also vary with the contours of each nation's culture.

Japan: fewer deaths, fewer births

13

Will saving the lives of more children lead to more population growth, undermining economic progress and making it more difficult to improve incomes, health, and education?

Page 23 of this report argues that the opposite effect is more likely. But as a practical example, it is worth looking at what has actually happened in the country which has reduced child deaths more steeply than any other.

In 1940, Japan's infant mortality rate (IMR) was 90 deaths per 1,000 births – higher than most developing countries today. Today it is down to 5.5 – and Japan ranks alongside Finland and Sweden in having the lowest rate of infant deaths in the world.

With such a rapid drop in child deaths, what has happened to Japan's rate of population growth?

As in all nations, the initial result is an increase in the number of children who survive to have children of their own, and hence a temporary rise in population growth rates. But with growing confidence in the survival of their children, parents everywhere tend to have smaller families. In the Japan of 1940, the average number of children per couple was more than 4. By 1960 it was 2. Today it is 1.8. In demographic terms, Japan's parents are not even replacing themselves.

As for economic progress, few will need reminding that Japan has registered a higher annual rate of economic growth over the last four decades than any other nation on earth.

Obviously, many factors are involved in such a demographic and economic transition. Nonetheless, Japan's experience resoundingly contradicts the idea that reducing child deaths inevitably accelerates population growth and slows economic progress.

Falling child deaths and falling birth rates are both related to rising GNP. But as experience in of many nations shows, that link is neither inevitable nor automatic. In Japan, achievements in child health and survival have also been the result of a conscious effort to protect children – including the education of parents in modern methods of child care.

'Life improvement workers' (sekatsu kaizenin), for example, are attached to every agricultural cooperative, and their work in health and nutrition education has been a major factor in improving child survival and development.

For many years now, every pregnant woman in Japan has been given a 'mother and child notebook' (boshi techo) which is kept at home as a source of advice on her own and her child's progress. The first few pages record the mother's weight gain and blood pressure in pregnancy and urge her to come to 'mother's classes'. The classes themselves teach the essentials of child care and, for every class completed, the techo is stamped at the local health centre. With its front-cover message – "Take good care of this book until your child enters school" – the notebook also contains the child's birth-weight, immunization record, growth chart, a check-list on physical and mental development, and advice about protecting the nutritional health of a child under five years old.

In other words, a conscious effort has been made to empower Japanese parents with the knowledge and the means to protect their children's health. The success of this effort has both contributed to, and benefited from, Japan's achievements in slowing population growth and accelerating economic growth. And it is a pattern which can also be detected in those developing countries which have seen rapid rates of growth in per capita GNP during the 1980s – China, Thailand, Singapore, Sri Lanka, and the Republic of Korea. Like Japan, all of these nations have invested heavily, and at an early stage, in the education and health of their children – and achieved steep falls in child death rates.

The constant element is that any individual or organization that can in any way help to inform and support parents in applying such knowledge is now a potentially important resource for promoting the health of the nation's children. That is the underlying principle of social mobilization. And it is a dynamic application of primary health care's most fundamental tenet – that health is the responsibility not just of the medical profession but of society as a whole.

Within the limits of generalization across countries and cultures, it is therefore time to be specific about the partners who could now play a part in the Grand Alliance for Children.

Educators

There are more than five times as many teachers in the developing world as there are health workers. They usually see more of families with young children and their contact with pupils is long-term and regular rather than fleeting and infrequent. Eighty per cent of the developing world's children now enrol in school, and 60% complete at least four years. The formal education system is therefore the developing world's broadest and deepest channel for putting information at the disposal of its citizens.

Efforts have been and are being made to put health education onto the syllabus. But the scale of that effort is in no way proportionate to its potential. And the case should now be made to ministers of education, to school principals, to teachers, to the heads of training colleges, to the publishers of textbooks, that *no child should leave school without today's knowledge about protecting the lives and the normal mental and physical growth of children.*

Some nations are already seizing this opportunity. In *Turkey* this year, the 200,000 teachers who helped to organize the nation's vaccination campaign are now being trained in today's basic child health knowledge. In *Thailand*, similar lessons are being put before 6.3 million children through the standard school curriculum. In *Ecuador*, 34,000 teachers and 150,000 secondary-school students have this year been given a week's training in child health. In *Kenya*, basic child health messages are being included in the reformed primary-school curriculum. And in the *Middle East*, WHO and UNESCO are co-operating with governments to launch a joint Health Education Curriculum Development Programme for 25 million primary-school children.

Such efforts clearly have a double value. In the long term, reaching the majority of today's schoolchildren means reaching the majority of tomorrow's parents. Says the Director of WHO's Expanded Programme on Immunization (EPI), "*If we had started in all schools in 1974 when EPI began, we could have got the immunization message to most of those who are becoming parents today.*" In the shorter term, schoolchildren themselves can be a channel for putting health knowledge at the disposal of their own families and communities.

In some countries, that potential is now being institutionalized. To graduate from secondary school in *Colombia* today, for example, students not only have to know about basic child protection methods, they also have to spend 30 hours in community service to put that knowledge at the disposal of families (panel 5).

Educators and teachers know how to communicate with their students. Will they now use that power to communicate today's child health knowledge to the next generation of parents?

Business and labour

Employers and trade unions are in regular contact with literally hundreds of millions of parents in the developing world. The retail, service, and advertising professions also communicate with the general public.

Businessmen and labour leaders could therefore make a crucial contribution to the empowering of parents with today's knowledge.

Many employers and union officials, worldwide, are already involved in important health issues such as the right to maternity leave and the provision of crèches and breast-feeding facilities in the work-place. Those issues are an ideal context for informing and supporting parents in

Self-health: the tobacco test

14

In the industrialized world, more and more people know that they can improve their chances of a long and healthy life by taking more responsibility for their own health. The guidelines are simple – don't smoke, don't get overweight, take regular exercise, and cut down on salt, sugar, saturated fats, cholesterol, and alcohol. But is this knowledge changing the way people behave?

So far, tobacco smoking has been the main testing ground for the idea that the promotion of knowledge can lead to improvements in health via changes in behaviour. And the evidence to date suggests that persistent public education can loosen even tobacco's addictive grip.

The message that smoking is responsible for 30% of all heart disease, 75% of bronchitis cases, and 90% of lung cancers, has been promoted through the health services, the schools, the media, the work-place, and by warnings on tobacco products and advertisements. The result is a slow but steady decline in smoking (see fig. 2). In Sweden, the proportion of male adults who smoke has fallen from 50% to under 30% in the last seven years. In the United Kingdom, the proportion has fallen from 65% in 1948 to 38% in 1982 and in the United States from 40% in 1978 to just over 30% today. And even in heavy-smoking Japan, the proportion of men who smoke has fallen from 83% in 1966 to 63% in 1986.

Despite a rise in tobacco smoking among women, and a failure to persuade a significant minority of the young, overall tobacco consumption is now declining by just over 1% per year in the industrialized world. And this has been achieved in the face of a $2 billion-a-year advertising campaign by the tobacco industry.

Because decades elapse before tobacco smoking shows up as lung cancer or heart disease, the benefits of these changes are not yet as easy to measure. But in the United States, age-specific lung cancer rates in men appear to be declining in proportion to the decline in smoking. And according to the American Heart Association, deaths from heart disease among men have also decreased significantly in recent years, "coinciding with a 25% decrease in the prevalence of smoking".

Similar patterns are emerging in other industrialized nations. In Canada, for example, WHO reports a decrease in heart disease and an increase in life expectancy attributed to "the fact that more and more Canadians have stopped smoking". In Europe, Finland and Belgium are leading the way with information and legislation against smoking. And in Japan, though the majority of men still smoke cigarettes, the first shots have been fired this year with no-smoking announcements by several major employers and department stores.

In some countries, a new momentum has come from the finding that non-smokers are also at risk from tobacco smoking in their immediate environment. US health groups now claim that this involuntary or 'secondary' smoking is responsible for at least 5,000 deaths a year and in December 1986 US Surgeon-General Everett Koop confirmed that "non-smokers are placed at increased risk".

Since Koop's announcement, there has been a further 8% drop in cigarette smoking in the United States, and, as *Time* magazine reported in February 1987, "every week brings new rules and a new tightening of old rules" in what has become a "nation-wide crusade against smoking". No-smoking signs have now gone up in all 6,800 US government buildings to clear the air for 1 million federal employees.

In support of such efforts, the World Health Organization has announced that "nothing less than the removal of this man-made hazard would be compatible with the goal of Health for All by the year 2000" other crucial areas of child health action. But in some countries, both employers and unions have gone much further.

In *Thailand*, *Sri Lanka* and *Burkina Faso*, for example, trade unions have started their own child health seminars for their members. In the *Philippines*, women's trade unions have begun their own child health education programmes. In *Mexico*, sixty of the largest factories have introduced family planning programmes for their work-forces. In *Nicaragua*, union leaders are *ex officio* members of local health committees and take responsibility both for educating their own members in health matters and for enlisting their help with community health projects such as the organization of vaccination and malaria control, and the staffing of oral rehydration units.

But in most nations, what is being done is only a shadow of what could be done. All employers and all trade union leaders could be asked to make a long-term commitment to the task of ensuring that all of their employees and all of their members will be empowered with basic child health knowledge within the next few years.

The means at their disposal are many – posters, videos, and public address announcements in work-places and canteens; regular messages in pay packets or on time-sheets; company mail systems, health worker visits, worker education courses.

In addition, those businesses which communicate directly with a large public could also use that opportunity to promote child health messages. In *Brazil* and *Colombia*, for example, information about the need for a full course of vaccines has reached millions of parents by being printed on bank statements and electricity bills, lottery tickets and carrier bags, commercial calendars and sponsored newspaper advertisements. This year, Dhaka Match Industries of *Bangladesh* has put immunization messages on 250 million of its matchboxes. The same could be done on till receipts and food packaging, advertisements and ration coupons, cinema screens and billboards.

Employers and trade unions, advertising agencies and marketing companies, know how to communicate with their employees, their custom-

ers, and their members. In the years ahead, will they too join an alliance to defend the lives and the normal development of their nation's children?

Organized religion

The voice of organized religion regularly reaches out to hundreds of millions of the developing world's parents both directly and via the print and electronic mass media. And the respect in which that voice is held gives it a special place in the alliance for child health.

Soon after the announcement by UNICEF in December 1982 of the potential for a revolution in child survival and development, the Holy See announced that "*the entire Catholic aid network in the various countries of the world ... will lend its maximum support to these important, simple proposals to improve the health of hundreds of millions of children*". The World Council of Churches has also voiced its support, and Islamic and Buddhist leaders have become directly involved in promoting child survival. In *Egypt*, for example, the prestigious University of Al Azar has researched messages from the Koran in support of immunization and child protection, and the Grand Sheik has asked that they be distributed to all Egyptian families via the mosques in each community.

In *Colombia*, Catholic priests in more than 2,000 parishes have preached the need for immunization on national vaccination days. In *Turkey*, the nation's 54,000 imams reached almost all parents with immunization messages in that country's recent campaign to immunize 80% of its children (panel 9). In *Sri Lanka*, Buddhist priests are bringing child survival messages to thousands of villages. In *Indonesia*, Islamic texts are reinforcing the effort to promote breast-feeding, improved child feeding, and growth monitoring. In Latin America, priests in some nations are beginning to use the traditional pre-marital and pre-baptism counselling sessions to inform couples about immunization, oral rehydration, and the value of breast-feeding and growth monitoring. In *Brazil*, the considerable power of the Catholic Church, with its 7,000 priests and many trained health workers, its 120 radio stations and hundreds of parish newspapers and magazines, has established a 'Pastorate of the Child' programme to bring today's child protection strategies to the families of 1 million young children nation-wide. In *El Salvador*, the Church has played a courageous role in helping to organize the three 'days of tranquillity' each year on which the fighting stops and the nation's children are immunized.

But over and above the support they can give to particular campaigns, religious leaders are in regular contact with probably a majority of the world's parents. And they too could make a long-term commitment to the task of empowering those parents with today's health knowledge.

Religious leaders know how to communicate to their own congregations. Will they now accept the challenge of joining a public health alliance to help protect today's children, and tomorrow's world?

The mass media

With 60% literacy, almost 4,000 daily newspapers, 400 million transistor radios (five times more than twenty years ago), 92 million television sets (eight times more than twenty years ago), the developing world can now communicate with the majority of its families via the print and electronic mass media (fig. 11).[24]

In the 1980s, this new communications muscle has strengthened virtually every successful attempt to put today's child health messages at the disposal of the majority of parents.

In *Syria* and in *Egypt*, national television personalities have brought the message about immunization and ORT into millions of homes. In *Brazil*, $6 million in air time has helped to promote information about breast-feeding to virtually every urban family. In *Turkey*, child health messages are a permanent feature on national radio and television and, so far, an estimated $5 million in air time has helped parents to bring most of the nation's children to be immunized. In *Mexico*, soap operas or *teleno-*

velas such as the *Acompañame* series have won wide acclaim for the integration of family planning and child health messages into their nightly dramas. In *Pakistan*, prime-time television pictures of children suffering from vaccine-preventable diseases have helped to significantly increase Karachi's immunization coverage. In *Nicaragua* and *Nepal*, tens of thousands of comic books, songs and poems have been produced on topics such as immunization, hygiene, and the prevention and treatment of diarrhoeal disease. In *Colombia*, leading newspapers and television and radio stations have covered the attempt to immunize the nation's children not just as a news story but as a *cause*, monitoring and relaying the results to the nation with an urgency usually reserved for the coverage of general elections.

But again, the contribution of the print and electronic mass media to an alliance for child health could go far beyond this support for individual campaigns. A majority of the developing world's parents could now be regularly reached with vital child health messages. And what is now needed is a *long-term commitment* by proprietors and editors, journalists and broadcasters, film-makers and cinema chains, to the task of ensuring that a majority of their readers and listeners and viewers will be empowered with today's child health knowledge.

Those who own and those who run the television networks, the radio stations, the cinema and video chains, the newspapers and magazines, know how to communicate with their audiences. As a tangible expression of their social responsibility, will they too now use that power to help promote the health of their nations' children?

Voluntary agencies

Internationally, over 3,000 non-governmental organizations are now working to improve the quality of life in the developing world. Together, they spend approximately $3.5 billion a year, between a third and a half of it on health.[25] Nationally, there are now countless numbers of voluntary agencies (an estimated 12,000 in India alone) and many of them are working in communities where the need is greatest.

Fig. 11 Number of television sets and radio receivers in the developing world per 1,000 inhabitants, 1965–1983

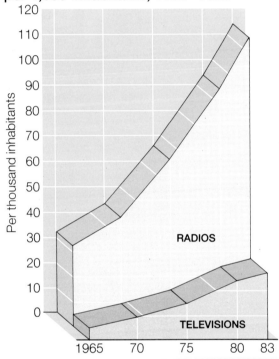

The developing world's capacity to communicate has been transformed in recent years. Radio now reaches a majority of families, television a majority of communities.

Source: UNESCO Statistical Yearbook, 1986.

Voluntary organizations could therefore reach into a majority of communities with the child health information which every family now has a right to know. And in recent years, many of those organizations have been involved in pioneering both the knowledge itself and the ways and means of putting it at the disposal of the majority.

In *Indonesia*, for example, 12 religious organizations have launched a joint communications programme, using regular religious channels including study groups, prayer meetings, and home visits, in order to enhance the child survival knowledge of 10 million mothers by the end of 1988.

In *Sri Lanka*, 4,000 volunteers of the Sarvo-daya movement are working with mothers' groups (*mavu havulas*) in 3,500 villages to popularize health knowledge, including knowledge of ORT, and to help organize immunization programmes. Another medical voluntary agency, the Sankyadana movement, has enlisted the support of 1,000 Buddhist priests and trained over 2,000 volunteers to advise communities on immunization, coping with diarrhoeal disease, improving hygiene, and monitoring child growth.

In *India*, the Voluntary Health Association of India works with over 3,000 organizations to provide training and health care to some of the poorest communities on the subcontinent.

Major international non-governmental organizations have also been in the vanguard of this movement. Since 1984, the Red Cross and Red Crescent Societies, with a global network of 230 million members, have been working under the slogan of 'Child alive' to put today's knowledge about oral rehydration therapy and diarrhoeal disease control at the disposal of millions of parents. Similarly, the Scout and Guide movement, with 25 million members in over 150 countries, has launched a 'Help children grow' programme by which Scouts and Guides both learn and teach the techniques of ORT and the importance of immunization, breast-feeding, and growth monitoring. In support of polio immunization, Rotary International has launched its massive world-wide 'Polio Plus' campaign which aims to raise $120 million to help eradicate poliomyelitis.

The various national family planning organizations, the Save the Children Federation, the Christian Medical Commissions, the Aga Khan Foundation, Catholic Relief Services, CARE, the Oxfams of various nations, and many more voluntary organizations are involved in some of today's most successful child health programmes.

Through such organizations, members of the public in both industrialized and developing countries have an opportunity to play a part in the alliance for child health. Will they now use that opportunity to invest their time, their talents, and their money in helping parents to use today's knowledge to protect the lives and the normal development of their children?

SAARC:
children first

15

Traditionally, developing countries have formed regional associations mainly for trade and economic co-operation. But in the mid-1980s, regional organizations in Africa, Central America, and South Asia have begun building a concern for their region's children into their political agendas.

The seven nations of the recently formed South Asian Association for Regional Co-operation (SAARC) – Bangladesh, Bhutan, India, Maldives, Nepal, Pakistan, and Sri Lanka – are home to 400 million children under the age of five. Each year, another 34 million infants are born. Of those, 4 million do not survive to reach their first birthday and another 2 million die before they are five. Not all of those who survive grow up to fulfil their potential and to become healthy, productive adults.

Even allowing for the variations within and between the nations of this vast region, the health problems faced by its children are largely common problems – an interactive cluster of infections and malnutrition, illiteracy and exploitation. All the SAARC nations can therefore gain by sharing their experience in improving the lives of their children.

But only if it ranks high on political agendas will such co-operation be effective. In November 1986, SAARC's first summit meeting issued the Bangalore Declaration, in which "the heads of state or government recognized that the meeting of the needs of all children was the principal means of human resource development. Children should therefore be given the highest priority in national development planning."

Making this more specific, the seven heads of state committed themselves to the goals of universal immunization by 1990 and, by the year 2000, universal primary education, adequate maternal and child nutrition, safe drinking water and adequate shelter for all.

The summit was preceded by a SAARC-sponsored South Asian Conference on Children which, with the participation of UNICEF, made detailed recommendations on how those objectives might be achieved. At the summit itself, the heads of state set up a standing committee of the seven nations' foreign secretaries "to undertake annual reviews of the situation of the children in SAARC countries, monitor programmes and exchange experiences". In other words, a mechanism is now in place which both mirrors and maintains the new political priority being accorded to children's needs.

To give technical support, a secretariat for SAARC has been established in Kathmandu. Specialist committees on health and population, and on women and development, have included children's concerns in their activities. Other committees are also being asked to build the needs of the child into their work on SAARC's wider goals such as co-operation in agricultural development and in science and technology.

To deepen support for SAARC's aims, groups of advocates and activists for children are also being formed among parliamentarians, professional associations, writers and artists, business interests and institutions, and among the region's many voluntary organizations.

Given this political climate, there are today two main sources of new hope for South Asia's children. First, there is a consensus among the region's political leaders that economic progress has largely neglected human development and that investment in the physical and mental development of children is an essential long-term investment in the social and economic development of nations. Second, the progress which South Asia has made in so many other directions in recent years means that it now has the resources – material, technical, and institutional – to give practical substance to any political decision to improve the protection afforded to the region's children. If those resources are mobilized in that cause, then the year 1995 could see a halving of the 1985 child death rate in all countries of the region.

That alliance of peoples and voluntary organizations is also capable of crossing political chasms. In September 1986, for example, youth delegates from East and West, including representatives of the Boy Scouts and the Young Pioneers, met at Erevan in the Soviet Union. There, in the 'spirit of Erevan', they emphasized their agreements, set aside their differences, and made known their views on the major problems facing the world's children.

Medical services

There are now approximately 2 million doctors and 6 million trained nurses and midwives in the developing nations, more than double the number of ten or fifteen years ago. And since the International Conference on Primary Health Care held at Alma-Ata in the Soviet Union in 1978, many millions of community health workers have been trained to serve in the villages and neighbourhoods of the poor world. In India alone, approximately 200,000 *anganwadi* workers have been trained to inform and support parents in child care.[26] As a result, some kind of modern health care is now available to the majority of parents, albeit with varying degrees of expertise and accessibility (fig. 13).

More will be said in a moment about the anchor role of the community health worker. But doctors and clinics, by the scale of their outreach and the influence of their status, also have a major part to play in informing and supporting parents in using today's knowledge.

Every contact between clinic or health worker and parent and child, no matter what the immediate reason for the consultation, is an opportunity to inform and to reassure parents about such vital and basic things as breast-feeding, birth spacing, immunization, weaning, growth checking, and oral rehydration. *"Every time a mother and child come to a clinic or health centre,"* says Dr. Ralph Henderson, Director of the WHO Expanded Programme on Immunization, *"a doctor or health worker should go through a basic health and growth check, a questioning and a strengthening of the mother's knowledge about the basic things which a parent can do to promote a child's normal healthy growth."*

But by and large, that opportunity is being missed.

It is being missed because the medical establishment in most nations is structured and trained and staffed for dealing with illness rather than promoting health.

It is being missed because a majority of health professionals are behind the times in their knowledge of oral rehydration or breast-feeding or growth monitoring.

It is being missed because most medical professionals receive no meaningful training in communications skills, despite the fact that effective communication is probably the most important contribution they can make to public health.

It is being missed because of the prevailing notion that health is something to be actively delivered by experts and passively received by the public. The basic determinants of a child's health are in the hands of parents, not doctors. And only if there is an about-face in attitudes and training, only if medical professionals see their task as one of demystifying their medical knowledge and empowering others to use it, will they make their potential contribution to the advance in child health which is now possible.

Indirectly, also, all health professionals communicate to a larger public than they will ever meet. If paediatricians in maternity wards institute rooming-in of new-born babies with their mothers, banish feeding-bottles, and encourage mothers to breast-feed, then they are making a statement which will be heard well beyond the walls of the hospital (panel 12). If doctors both use and teach oral rehydration therapy, rather than prescribing anti-diarrhoeal drugs, then they will be reinforcing rather than contradicting the efforts of schools, or mass media, or religious leaders, to promote a therapy which is not only the cheapest way of dealing with childhood's most common illness, but also the best.

There is now increasing evidence that the medical profession, whose expertise must guide this world-wide alliance, is beginning to bring its weight behind the idea of empowering parents with today's health knowledge. The International Paediatric Association, for example, has announced that it is now possible to reduce disease and death among the world's children by half within the next decade and called upon all its member organizations, and all individual paediatricians, to join in the effort. The Indian Medical Association has made a commitment to retrain its membership of 70,000 doctors in the use of oral therapy. The Nigerian Medical Association has also recently issued a statement on the importance of "*disseminating current information on these strategies to all doctors, nurses, pharmacists, and other cadres of health staff as well as to the community at large*".

Similarly, the International Council of Nurses and the International Confederation of Midwives have given their moral and practical support. And under the auspices of the United States Agency for International Development (USAID), two major international conferences on oral rehydration therapy have brought together medical researchers and practitioners from all regions of the world to share experiences and plan the promotion of the new therapy.

The health profession, from the medical colleges to the rural clinics, directly or indirectly influences the health attitudes and behaviour of almost all parents. And its knowledge and prestige can be used either to promote dependence on the medical mystique or to empower people with the knowledge and confidence to take more responsibility for their own and their families' health (fig. 12).

The public role

In both developing and industrialized nations, members of the public can also play a part by supporting the many voluntary agencies which are now involved in the struggle to realize today's potential for saving the lives and protecting the growth of children. But there is also a broader role to be played in influencing the policies of governments which provide the framework for that struggle.

Mention has already been made of the support from the governments of such countries as Italy, the United States, Sweden and Canada. In all of these cases, public concern, expressed in thousands of newspaper editorials, letters to the editor, and responses to appeals, has played an important part. But there is an ever broader role, in all industrialized nations, for an informed public questioning of government policies on aid and trade and debts. Pages 23 to 31 of this report have described how present economic policies threaten both past progress and present potential for advances in child health. To ward off that threat, there is a need for steady public pressure to ensure that all countries now making genuine efforts to protect the living standards of the poorest families are helped rather than hindered in that struggle by the international community.

That support may sometimes take a form which seems a long way removed from the subject of child health. It may mean support for debt relief and restructuring, or for increases in real aid and a renewal of loans, or for restrictions on arms sales and a lifting of trade barriers against manufactured goods. But these are matters of legitimate concern for UNICEF and all who wish to see an end to unnecessary suffering among the world's young children. For in its day-to-day work, UNICEF sees too often how short a step it can be from a balance-of-payments crisis to a shortage of essential drugs, from a rise in oil prices to a mobile vaccination unit without fuel, from a debt falling due to a clinic being closed, from the withdrawal of a food subsidy to the stunting of a child.

The appeal to all

This sketch of the range of social resources which could be mobilized to inform and support parents is intended to stimulate rather than to limit the imagination which now needs to be brought to bear on this task. Organized sports, leisure, and entertainment, for example, can also reach out to millions of families. People's own organizations, whether they be peasant co-operatives, neighbourhood associations, consumer organizations, women's groups, or professional associations, also have a part to play.* And government employees and agencies of all kinds, be they departments of family planning, water and sanitation, agricultural extension, or even the police and tax collection forces, reach out regularly to large numbers of people and are therefore also a communications resource.

---

* In recent years, the poor in many nations have become increasingly reachable through their own organizations such as the Working Women's Forum in Madras (50,000 members), the Self-Employed Women's Association of Gujarat (15,000 members), the Grameen Bank groups in Bangladesh (100,000 members), and the Working Women's Savings Clubs in Zimbabwe (200,000 members).

In sum, it is not only the knowledge to improve family health that is now available. The social resources to put that knowledge at the disposal of the majority are also in place. But for the one to serve the other, the whole of society must accept a larger share of responsibility for the health of its children. For it is nothing less than a *permanent social mobilization* which could now transform what *can* now be done into what *will* now be done.

It is a lot to ask. And all of these possible participants already have their own agendas and priorities. But the basis of the appeal to all sections of society is simply that there is no greater cause in which to march.

Fig. 12 Increase in mothers' knowledge of treating diarrhoeal disease, Egypt, 1984–1985

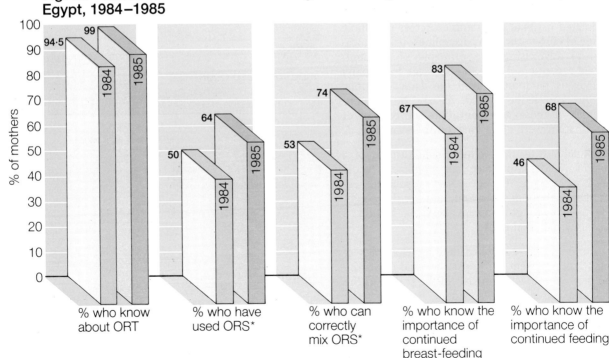

The commitment of Egypt's medical and mass media professionals has empowered the majority of Egypt's mothers with the knowledge to prevent the death and malnutrition caused by diarrhoeal dehydration. One result is a significant reduction in dehydration deaths, which used to claim the lives of up to 130,000 Egyptian children each year.

* ORS = oral rehydration solution (available in 5.5 gramme packets from government health centres and most pharmacies).
Source: National Surveys reported in draft MOH/USAID/UNICEF/WHO Evaluation Report, 1986.

For it can no longer be considered acceptable, in a world which has any pretensions to civilization, that so many millions of children should be dying, and that so many millions more should be stunted and blinded and brain-damaged, because the world has neglected to fully inform and support their families in today's practical and affordable ways of protecting children's lives and growth.

Another child will die in the time it takes to read this sentence. And the death of that child, a child who had a name and a personality, a family and a future, is a rebuke to all humanity. It is no longer necessary. It should therefore no longer be acceptable.

Political will

Almost any organized resource can therefore now become involved in this cause. But the efforts of all will be multiplied if they are part of a co-ordinated national programme. Across the whole range of communications disciplines, from education to advertising, the principle of frequent, varied repetition of the same message from many sources is paramount. And the flame of public health knowledge would clearly burn more brightly if those who contribute the oxygen of information were all to blow on the same fire.

Usually, it is the political commitment of a nation's leadership which can mobilize a whole society, procure the necessary resources, co-ordinate supply and demand, and put the weight of permanent government services behind a sustained national effort.

Although there are outstanding examples of such commitment, it must be said that the political will to act on behalf of the poor and the vulnerable is not always evident. And across the whole spectrum of the development effort, the failure to transform plans into progress, and potential into achievement, is most often put down to the missing magic ingredient – political will.

This lack is not exclusively the fault of politicians, and needs to be tackled not as some insuperable hurdle but as yet another obstacle

which must somehow be overcome. And it is becoming increasingly clear that political commitment *can* be elicited, in varying degrees, if humanitarian appeals are framed in such a way as to also make financial and political sense. Experts in health and other fields of social development need to shape and simplify their expertise into plans which are practical and affordable, with obvious starting-points and attainable objectives, and to present those plans in such a way as to

Fig. 13 Availability of health care for pregnant women and infants, 1986*

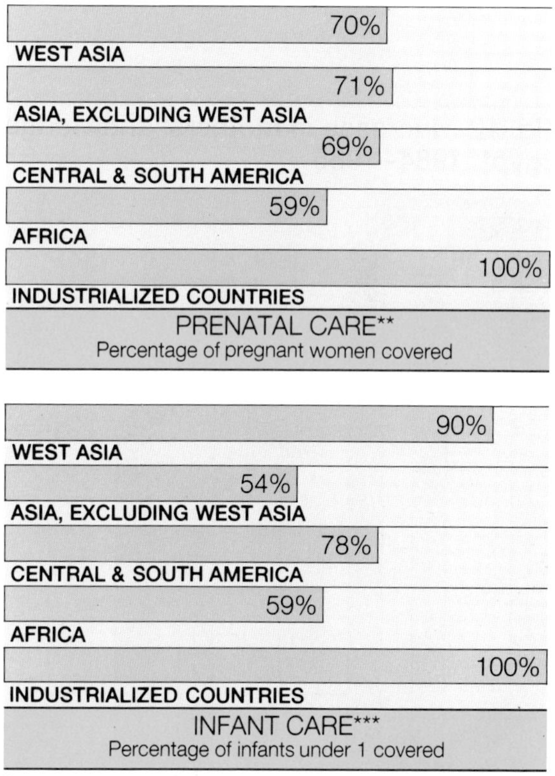

PRENATAL CARE**
Percentage of pregnant women covered

WEST ASIA	70%
ASIA, EXCLUDING WEST ASIA	71%
CENTRAL & SOUTH AMERICA	69%
AFRICA	59%
INDUSTRIALIZED COUNTRIES	100%

INFANT CARE***
Percentage of infants under 1 covered

WEST ASIA	90%
ASIA, EXCLUDING WEST ASIA	54%
CENTRAL & SOUTH AMERICA	78%
AFRICA	59%
INDUSTRIALIZED COUNTRIES	100%

Care for pregnant mothers and children under one is now available to a majority of families in the developing world.

*Trained personnel available and can be reached in no more than one hour by the usual local means of transport (including walking).
** 101 countries, excluding China, Nigeria, and Bangladesh.
*** 72 countries, excluding China, Nigeria, Brazil, India, and Bangladesh.

*Sources: Health care availability: World Health Organization.
1986 population: UN Population Division and UNICEF estimates.*

capture the imagination of both politicians and public. To realize the present potential, nation-wide action for children can be, and must be seen to be, *good politics.*

The weakness, indeed sometimes the lack, of commitment among ruling élites to the well-being of the majority has been and still is a major obstacle to development in many nations. And the struggle for leadership in the interests of the poor majority is and should be a permanent feature of the development process. But all improvement cannot wait upon political utopia. And side by side with that struggle, there is also a need to formulate proposals which are capable of capturing political will and translating it into social improvement.

Involving a wide variety of communications resources in achieving great national goals which are close to the hearts of the majority is a contribution to society which does make political sense. It can bring measurable results in the immediate future without making impossible demands on available resources. It is by far the most cost-effective investment which can be made in the nation's social and economic future. And it improves the lives of children *today.*

The question must therefore also be put to a nation's leaders. In the years immediately ahead, will they lead an alliance for health by making a personal and political commitment to reducing child deaths and child malnutrition on the scale that is now possible?

Support for women

Even with the political will to do what can now be done, the knowledge road to health still has many pitfalls.

The wide variety of communications channels already discussed will not easily reach those who are illiterate and unemployed, those who do not own a television or a radio, those whose children do not go to school and whose social status effectively prevents their participation in many of the organizations through which they might be reached. And even if this problem of outreach can be solved, by using all possible ingenuity and every possible channel, there remains the less tangible problem of the poor self-image, the lack of confidence in change, the sense of power-lessness, which is born of long years of poverty and oppression.

These two problems are further compounded by the fact that it is also the very poorest who face the greatest practical and external difficulties in putting new knowledge into action. Those who are not educated cannot easily read reminders about the time and place of immunization. Those who live without water supply or sanitation do not find it easy to keep dirt and flies away from homes and food and water. Those who must work all day in fields or factories cannot always breast-feed an infant or provide freshly cooked food four or five times a day for a young child.

Yet it is among the poorest that the need is greatest. The poorer the family, the greater the likelihood and the risks of low birth-weight and malnutrition, of diarrhoeal disease and respira-tory infection, of poor growth and early death. Therefore the obstacles must, somehow, be overcome.

In recent years, it has been shown that very poor and often uneducated parents can and will put today's child health information into action – if all possible channels are used to inform and

The Convention: rights of the child

16

As far back as Roman times, the law treated children as parental – usually paternal – property. Not until the 19th century did children begin to be recognized as requiring special protection to limit the exploitation of child labour, to provide basic education, to ensure some form of financial support for the most dependent, and to prevent extreme cases of neglect and abuse.

The 20th century has seen this principle extended internationally. In 1924, the Geneva Declaration stated that "the child deserves the best mankind has to give" – and today there are more than 80 international laws, covenants, and declarations setting out 'human rights for children'.

Since 1980, a working group of the Human Rights Commission has been drafting a Convention on the Rights of the Child, drawing together those existing and some new international duties and obligations into a comprehensive legal instrument intended to be binding on all nations which accept it.

Given an extraordinary effort in 1988, the Convention could be finalized in time to be formally presented to the General Assembly of the United Nations in 1989 – the tenth anniversary of the International Year of the Child.

The difference is the binding nature of a Convention's provisions on all ratifying nations. Many of the existing documents are not legally enforceable, many simply a declaration of principle. This will be the first time that these rights have been brought together in one Convention which, once accepted, has the force of a binding obligation.

It is this rigour which makes agreement on the provisions of a Convention such a meticulous, time-consuming process. Members of the Working Group represent their countries and thus their national as well as international concerns.

The draft Convention consists of 35 articles covering civil, political, economic, social and cultural rights ranging from 'survival' rights, such as adequate health care, food, clean water, and shelter, to rights of protection against abuse, neglect and exploitation; the right to safe and proper development through formal education; and freedom to participate in the social, economic, religious, and political life of their culture.

The Convention and the rights it sets out are based on three principles: that children need special safeguards beyond those provided to adults; that the best environment for a child's survival and development is within a protective and nurturing family setting; and that governments, and the adult world in general, should be committed to acting in the best interests of children.

Governments which formally accept and sign the Convention would have the responsibility of living up to its provisions and reflecting these in their own laws and regulations. Mechanisms for monitoring and reporting on the implementation of these provisions at the national level are still being discussed by the Working Group. One proposal is for a technical assistance mechanism to help requesting nations strengthen their own legislation and physical capacity to comply with the provisions of the Convention.

Concern about, and support for, the rights of the child has been growing steadily in this century – nationally and internationally – as industrialization and urbanization have put traditional social fabrics and certitudes under increasing and often intolerable strain – with many millions of children no longer able to count on their families for all the support they need. The Convention on the Rights of the Child is the most powerful international reflection of this concern and the most determined effort yet to do something about it.

support them in doing so.* But success in reaching the poorest – both with information and with practical and on-the-spot support in using it – is made much more likely with the support of one great resource which has not so far been discussed – the community health worker.

Community health workers

With approximately three months' training, a community health worker can give advice and help with birth spacing and pre-natal care, safe delivery and breast-feeding, disease prevention and immunization services, oral rehydration therapy and coping with diarrhoeal disease, basic home hygiene and adequate feeding, knowing what to do about acute respiratory infections and malaria, distributing vitamin A capsules and iron or iodine supplements, and helping with the regular growth monitoring of young children. In other words, a community health worker can help to root today's basic child health care knowledge in a community.

If that health worker is also a part of the community and its culture, then he or she is likely to know how best to adapt and communicate health information. That knowledge is vital. The poor are not empty vessels into which information can simply be poured. They have their own knowledge and their own beliefs about sickness, and that knowledge is often inseparable from the cultural and economic life of the community. Sensitive, respectful and effective communication is one of the most needed but most neglected of skills in development and the most important part of the community health worker's task.

The cost of training such a person – and people with little formal education have been taught to give this kind of support with great success – can be less than one fiftieth of the cost of training and equipping a fully qualified doctor. It is therefore not inconceivable that, within the next few years, every village and neighbourhood could be served by such a health worker. Some nations are already nearing that goal. And this growing army of community health workers could become the force for *health promotion* which has been so lacking in the make-up of most health services to date.

Today's knowledge equips health workers with powerful weapons against most of the main causes of ill health and poor growth. It therefore helps to establish their credibility in the eyes of the communities they serve. And if properly trained and supported, community health workers can refer more difficult questions to more qualified levels of the health service, so acting as the mechanism by which limited resources are deployed most efficiently in bringing the appropriate level of health care to each health problem.

The village or neighbourhood health worker is therefore a key to unlocking the potential of today's health knowledge. But he or she cannot work in a vacuum. And the more the infrastructure of primary health care is strengthened to support such workers, the more successful and durable will be the effort to put today's vital child health information at the disposal of all parents.

More public and political recognition and support is therefore the due of all those who now work to improve the health of the poor at all levels of today's precarious primary health care structures, whether they be nurses, midwives, doctors, water and sanitation workers, organizers of vaccination and diarrhoeal disease programmes, employees of government and national and international organizations, or any other individuals or organizations who have made it their priority to help protect the health of the poor.

It is they who battle on, often with little in the way of reward or acclaim, in the face of the non-arrival of supplies, or the non-payment of salaries, or the frustrations of bureaucratic inertia, or the mundane details of day-to-day difficulties. It is

---

* See, for example, panel 16, page 40, *The State of the World's Children 1985*, Oxford University Press.

Also, it should not be forgotten that reaching the not-quite-so-poor is in itself a way of putting information at the disposal of the very poorest. If the better-off families in a village or neighbourhood use oral rehydration therapy rather than anti-diarrhoeal drugs, breast-feed rather than bottle-feed, enrol for pre-natal care and plan their families, immunize their children and monitor their growth, then they are regularly communicating those messages to all other families in their communities.

Southern Africa: hidden casualties

17

The direct effects of apartheid on the children of South Africa have made the news in most nations in 1987. Less has been heard of the indirect effects of the apartheid conflict on the 15 million young children of the nine neighbouring states – Angola, Botswana, Lesotho, Malawi, Mozambique, Swaziland, Tanzania, Zambia and Zimbabwe.

In the most severely affected countries, economic disruption and military activities have increased child death rates by an estimated 75%. Mozambique and Angola, in particular, have seen their child death rates rise to among the highest in the world.

While drought, floods, falling trade, and past domestic policies have all contributed to this crisis, a 1987 report for UNICEF concludes that "the main culprits are war and economic pressure."

Hardest hit are Angola and Mozambique. Ever since achieving independence from Portugal in 1975, both countries have been beset by internal fighting and external attacks. Nonetheless, both countries had made an impressive start in mother and child care, immunization, essential drugs, drinking water supplies, and food availability for the poorest.

But with the beginning of the 1980s came a stepping up of externally-supported disruption, and among the casualties have been the frail structures of health and education. In Mozambique, for example, 585 health posts and health centres – almost half the total – have been destroyed since 1982. Over a third of all schools have also been wrecked or abandoned, leaving more than 500,000 primary-school children without education.

"One of the deadliest weapons of the war," says the report, "is the mass terrorism carried out by forces which have burned crops and farmhouses, pillaged and destroyed schools, clinics, churches, mosques, stores and villages, poisoned wells by throwing bodies down them, and attacked the transport system, which is a vital part of rural life."

Health workers, schoolteachers and pupils, foreign aid personnel, and vehicles transporting medical supplies and food have all been attacked with the aim of making large areas ungovernable. Power plants, ports and railway lines have also been targeted, along with tea estates, mines, cement plants and petroleum installations.

The costs of all this have also helped to sabotage services for mothers and children. Since 1980, losses caused by the military and economic struggle over apartheid are estimated at $17 billion for Angola, $5.5 billion for Mozambique, and $5 billion for the other seven states of the region.

The direct human costs of warfare amount to at least 100,000 deaths in Angola and Mozambique alone. But most of the region's deaths are not caused by weapons. They are caused by malnutrition and diarrhoea, by untreated respiratory infections, and by diseases which could have been prevented by immunization.

Health policies in Angola and Mozambique, during the late 1970s, looked likely to reduce under-five death rates to below 200 per 1,000 births (Tanzania's present level, for example, is 185 per 1,000). Instead, the rate in both countries has now risen to at least 325 per 1,000. It can therefore be estimated that approximately 140,000 young children have died in Angola and Mozambique this last year simply as a result of the armed struggle. "Every four minutes," says the UNICEF report, "a small Angolan or Mozambican child was lost who otherwise would have lived."

Peace, and an end to apartheid, are the prerequisites for both health and development in southern Africa. In the meantime, millions of children could be saved from the worst consequences of the conflict if the international community were to provide urgently needed finance, food, drugs, vaccines, transport, water supplies and help for improving food production.

they who carry on doing what they can when political change disrupts the steady progress that has been made or when the notice arrives from the ministry of finance to say that all budgets are being cut by 25% because of a fall in oil revenue, or a rise in interest rates, or a slump in raw material prices. And it is they who deal with the logistics of supply and transport, the problems of management and communication, the shortages of kerosene or cash.

And when the excitement and the publicity accompanying a national vaccination campaign has died down, when the memory of the encouraging words from the head of state is fading like the posters on the walls, it is they who must get on with the permanent job of maintaining the 'cold chain' and the sterilization equipment, the vaccine supplies and the information flow, so that immunization levels can be sustained for children not yet born.

The strengthening of primary health care structures, at all levels, is therefore a crucial test of a nation's political commitment to the health of the majority.

But in concluding this report, a report which has taken as its single theme the mobilization of all possible resources to do what can now be done to protect the lives and growth of their children, it must be said that the other crucial test of that commitment is the support which is given to its most important health workers of all – the nation's mothers.

Everyday hardship

In practice, it will usually be the mother who will decide such matters as whether to breast-feed and for how long, when to introduce other foods and how to prepare them, whether to add oil to gruel or give fluids when the child has diarrhoea, whether to take a child to be immunized or to regularly check its growth.

The realization of today's potential therefore comes down to a thousand small, everyday, almost unnoticed actions by many millions of mothers in poor communities throughout the world. A significant improvement in the state of the world's children therefore depends most of all on the state of the world's mothers – on their physical health and mental well-being, on their time and their energy, on their access to information and income, on their status and their morale.

It is therefore the mothers who will normally be the focus of the information and support which a society can summon – from husbands and families, from neighbours and communities, from health workers and clinics, from the media and the schools, from employers and labour unions, from religious and community leaders, from government services and development planners, and, not least, from the international community.

At the moment, that support is often weak or non-existent.* And the everyday hardship and discrimination which women face – in food, in education, in health care, in work, and in rewards – is today the single most important barrier to the improvement of their own and their children's health. With less education and status, less access to technology or training, and fewer resources of either cash or credit, women in almost all communities are expected to be not only wives and mothers but dutiful daughters and daughters-in-law, farmers and income-earners, home-makers and health workers, fuel-gatherers and animal-feeders, food-providers and water-carriers.

It is too much. And that is why the greatest communications challenge, for the wide range of aims and social resources discussed in this report, is the challenge of promoting the idea that society must give more support to its women, that their knowledge and skills should be afforded more recognition, and that men should also share more fully in the task of protecting the lives and the normal physical, mental and emotional growth of their children.

---

* The statistical tables in this year's *State of the World's Children* report include a new table of indicators on female equality and well-being, documenting such factors as female school enrolment as a percentage of male, percentage of births attended by trained personnel, etc.

Africa: the Bamako initiative

18

African health ministers meeting in Bamako, Mali, in September 1987, and joined by the Director-General of WHO and the Executive Director of UNICEF, have agreed on a major new initiative for achieving universal primary health care for women and children. The mainspring of the initiative is a new way of funding and managing essential drugs for each community. The drugs, bought in bulk at low cost, would be sold at prices which, while much lower than the local retail cost, would be sufficient to finance not only the replenishment of the drugs themselves but also the development of district health services to the point at which maternal and child health care is available to all.

Despite continuing economic difficulties, many African leaders have shown their determination to maintain progress for children. Between 1984 and 1987, over 40 nations in Africa have accelerated their immunization programmes toward univeral immunization by 1990.

Many African countries have also expanded their networks of health centres and village health posts. But with continuing financial difficulties, health services often lack even the most basic medicines and the funds to meet salaries and routine running costs. As a result, staff become demoralized and lose the confidence of the community.

Experience shows that most people are prepared to pay for medicines. Most rural people already pay far more than they should for irregular supplies of often inappropriate drugs. The problem is that no permanent system has been established for bringing good quality drugs to the community at low cost. That is exactly what the 'Bamako Initiative' aims to do.

Programmes supported by UNICEF and WHO and funded by several donor agencies in such countries as Kenya, Mozambique and Tanzania have shown that some 30 essential drugs can be regularly supplied to rural communities at a cost of less than 50 US cents per person per year.

The feasibility of a revolving fund for essential drugs has also been demonstrated by other projects. In one area of Benin (with a population of 15,000) generic drugs are bought through international organizations and sold, under community leadership and control, at a substantial mark-up (but still well below local retail prices). The community has adjusted prices to make preventive treatment free and exempted the poorest families from payment. Within three years, income from drug sales was not only replenishing the supply of drugs but also funding 85 percent of the local operating costs for primary health care – including village health workers' salaries and running costs.

The 'Bamako Initiative' envisages the spread of similar approaches – making maternal and child health care available across virtually the whole of Sub-Saharan Africa by the mid-1990s. External assistance for the initiative will be needed, rising to perhaps $100 million a year, if all countries join, before being phased down in the late 1990s as African governments themselves begin to cover more of the foreign exchange bill.

The beauty of the proposal lies in making primary health care far more self-sustaining at the community level. In addition to the value of the drugs themselves, reliable curative care builds the confidence of parents in the health services and complements efforts to promote other child health measures.

The initiative also provides a means for financing a continued flow of vaccines, syringes, and sterilization equipment to maintain universal child immunization in the 1990s. Strengthening district health services will also help in coping with the AIDS pandemic.

In July 1987 African Heads of State, meeting at the OAU Summit in Addis Ababa, declared 1988 the year for the protection, survival and development of African children. Discussions are now underway with several major donors who see the 'Bamako Initiative' as a way to give practical meaning to this declaration.

With the information and support which society could now put at the disposal of parents, the deaths of millions of children each year, and the malnutrition of many millions more, could be avoided. But all who march in that cause might bear in mind the words of the distinguished child psychologist Bruno Bettelheim who, after a lifetime spent working for disadvantaged children in the industrialized world, felt moved to say:-

"If I have any regret, it is that I did not emphasize sufficiently the difficulty which parents face. I saw my task to be the advocate of the child. But I believe now there is another important task – to be the advocate of the mother."

Conclusion

In conclusion, the essentials of the present opportunity should not be lost in the discussion of its many complexities. The handful of major threats to the lives and growth of the world's children could now be defeated, in large measure, by the emergence of a body of scientific information which almost all experts are agreed upon, which almost all parents can act upon, and which all governments could afford to facilitate even in the difficult economic times of the late twentieth century. At the same time, it has also become clear that putting this information at the disposal of all parents, and supporting them in using it, can only be achieved if a Grand Alliance of all possible social resources is mobilized to do it.

Five years ago, UNICEF said that if this 'social breakthrough' could be added to the 'knowledge breakthroughs' which were already available, then it would be possible to drastically reduce child deaths and child malnutrition throughout the world over the next decade. The scale of that potential may be broadly grasped by looking at the tragic figures with which this report began – the world-wide numbers of child deaths. In 1980, the death toll among the world's under-fives was approximately 43,000 per day. In 1987, that figure has been reduced to approximately 38,000 per day. And by 1990, it could and should be reduced to 33,000 per day or less. In other words, the potential of the child survival and development revolution, over the decade of the 1980s, is the *daily* saving of over 10,000 young lives.

The world is well started on the way to realizing this extraordinary potential. Basic low-cost measures such as ORT and immunization are already saving the lives of approximately 5,000 young children each day. But protecting the lives and the normal physical and mental growth of many millions of the world's children will remain a priority task for the remainder of this century. And both the failures and the successes to date have shown that the crucial element, if we are to succeed, is the participation of all possible resources in a Grand Alliance for Children.

All can therefore share in that task. All can play a part in the great gain for humanity which could now be made. All can now help to take this step towards a more genuinely civilized world.□

THE STATE OF THE WORLD'S CHILDREN 1988

Sources

1 United Nations Educational, Scientific and Cultural Organization (UNESCO) 1986.

2 *Child Survival: a second report to Congress on the AID program*, Agency for International Development, Washington DC. 1987.

3 World Health Organization, 1987.

4 Personal communication from Professor Chazov, Minister of Health of the USSR, 31 July 1987.

5 W.H. Foege and others, "Closing the Gap: report of The Carter Center Health Policy Consultation", *Journal of the American Medical Association*, September 1985, vol. 254, no. 10, pages 1355–1358.

6 Ralph H. Henderson, "Global overview: the Expanded Programme on Immunization", *Protecting the world's children*, "Bellagio II" at Cartagena, Colombia, The Task Force for Child Survival, October 1985, page 17.

7 R.H. Henderson, "Results of EPI sample surveys of immunization coverage performed during review of national programmes by year, 1978–1983", paper prepared for UNICEF, April 1984, supplemented by UNICEF field office reports, 1987.

8 Personal communication, Professor Mamdouh Gabr, Chairman, Department of Pediatrics, Cairo University, Egypt, May 1987.

9 "Health without wealth", *World Health Forum*, vol. 5, 1984, page 254.

10 United Nations Population Division and United Nations Statistical Office.

11 Giovanni Andrea Cornia, "Economic decline and human welfare in the first half of the 1980s", *Adjustment with a human face*, edited by Giovanni Cornia, Richard Jolly, and Frances Stewart, Oxford University Press, 1987, pages 11–47.

12 Gerry Helleiner and Frances Stewart, "The international system and the protection of the vulnerable", *Adjustment with a human face*, edited by Giovanni Cornia, Richard Jolly, and Frances Stewart, Oxford University Press, 1987, page 274.

13 Giovanni Cornia, "The Crisis of the Conventional Development Model in Latin America and Alternative Options for the Eradication of Poverty within the Present Adjustment Context", unpublished paper, 20 November 1986, page 2.

14 Gerry Helleiner and Frances Stewart, "The international system and the protection of the vulnerable", *Adjustment with a human face*, edited by Giovanni Cornia, Richard Jolly, and Frances Stewart, Oxford University Press, 1987, page 277.

15 B. Morse, "It can be done", *Development Forum*, vol. XIV, no. 5, June 1986, page 10.

16 H. Mahler quoted in Jill Turner, "A charter for health promotion", *The Lancet*, December 1986, page 1407.

17 "Healthier mothers and children through family planning", *Population reports*, series J, no. 27, May–June 1984. See also *World Fertility Survey; major findings and implications*, International Statistical Institute, 1984; and *Reproductive change in developing countries: insights from the world fertility survey*, edited by John Cleland and John Hobcraft, Oxford University Press, 1985, pages 24 and 290

18 World Health Organization, Division of Family Health. See also H. Mahler, "The safe motherhood initiative: a call to action", *The Lancet*, March 1987, pages 668–670.

19 "Breast-feeding, fertility and family planning", *Population Reports*, series J, no. 24, November–December 1981. See also Joe D. Wray, "Maternal nutrition, breast-feeding and infant survival", in W. Henry Mosley (ed.) *Nutrition and human reproduction*, Plenum Press 1978; and N.R. Clavano, "Mode of feeding and its effect on infant mortality and morbidity", Journal of Tropical Pediatrics, vol. 28, December 1982; and R.G. Feachem, "Non-clinical interventions for diarrhoea control: effectiveness and costs", paper presented at the Second International Conference on Oral Rehydration Therapy, Washington, December 1985, page 5.

20 R.H. Henderson, "Results of EPI sample surveys of immunization coverage performed during review of national programmes by year, 1978–1983", paper prepared for UNICEF, April 1984, supplemented by UNICEF field office reports, 1987.

21 WHO Programme for Control of Diarrhoeal Diseases, "Fourth Programme Report 1983–1984", 1985 (WHO/DCC/85.13). See also "Oral rehydration therapy (ORT) for childhood diarrhea", *Population Reports*, series L., no. 2, reprinted April 1982.

22 Leonardo Mata, "Control and prevention of diarrheal diseases at the national level", paper presented at the Second International Conference on Oral Rehydration Therapy, Washington, December 1985, page 1. See also Moslem Uddin Khan and Kamal Ahmad, "Withdrawal of food during diarrhoea: major mechanism of malnutrition following diarrhoea in Bangladesh children", *Journal of Tropical Pediatrics*, vol. 32. April 1986, page 60–61.

23 "Report of WHO/UNICEF Technical Inter-agency Meeting on acute Respiratory Infections", New York, March 1986, page 3. See also Antonio Pio, "Acute respiratory infections in children in developing countries: an international point of view", *Pediatric infectious disease*, vol. 5, no. 2, WHO, 1986, page 181; and *ARI news*, issue 3, AHRTAG, December 1985; and "Acute respiratory infections", progress report on WHO activities 1983–1984 and joint UNICEF–WHO statement on basic principles for control of acute respiratory infections in children in developing countries, Twenty-fifth session, Geneva January 1985.

24 United Nations Educational, Scientific and Cultural Organization.

25 Colette Braeckman, "NGOs: a new panacea?", *Development forum*, vol. XV, no. 2, March 1987, page 14.

26 *A decade of ICDS: integrated child development services*, Ministry of Human Resources Development (Department of Women's Welfare), Government of India. See also James P. Grant, "India: ICDS and the nation", *The state of the world's children*, Oxford University Press, 1987, page 36.

II

STATISTICS

Economic and social statistics on the
nations of the world, with particular
reference to children's well-being.

COUNTRY INDEX TO TABLES

TABLES

1: Basic Indicators
U5MR □ IMR □ population □ births and infant and child
deaths □ GNP per capita □ life expectancy □ adult literacy
□ school enrolment □ income distribution

2: Nutrition
Low birth-weight □ breast-feeding □ malnutrition □ food
production □ calorie intake

3: Health
Access to water □ access to health services □ immunization of
children and pregnant women □ production of ORS □ trained
attendance at birth □ maternal mortality

4: Education
Male and female literacy □ radio and television receivers □ primary school
enrolment and completion □ secondary school enrolment

5: Demographic Indicators
Child population □ population growth rate □ crude death rate
□ crude birth rate □ life expectancy □ fertility rate
□ urbanization □ contraceptive use

6: Economic Indicators
GNP per capita □ annual growth rates □ inflation □ poverty
□ government expenditure □ aid □ debts

7: Women
Life expectancy □ literacy □ enrolment in school □ contraceptive use
□ tetanus immunization □ trained attendance at births
□ maternal mortality

8: Basic Indicators for less populous countries
General note on the data
Signs and explanations
Footnotes for tables 1–8
Definitions
Main sources

General note on the data

The data provided in these tables are accompanied by definitions, sources, explanations of signs, and individual footnotes where the definition of the figure is different from the general definition being used. Tables derived from so many sources – nine major sources are listed in the explanatory material – will inevitably cover a wide range of reliability. Official government data received by the responsible United Nations agency have been used wherever possible. In the many cases where there are no reliable official figures, estimates made by the responsible United Nations agency have been used. Where such internationally standardized estimates do not exist, the tables draw on data from the relevant UNICEF field office. All data from UNICEF field office sources are marked with * or Y.

The figures for under-five and infant mortality rates, life expectancy, crude birth and death rates, etc., are part of the regular work on estimates and projections undertaken by the United Nations Population Division. These and other international estimates are revised periodically which explains why some of the data will differ from those found in earlier UNICEF publications. In the case of GNP per capita and ODA, the data are the result of a continuous process of revising and updating by the World Bank and OECD respectively.

Where possible only comprehensive or representative sample national data have been used although, as in the table on "Wasting", there are certain exceptions. Where the figures refer to only a part of the country, this is indicated in a footnote.

Signs and explanations

Unless otherwise stated, the summary measures for the four U5MR (under-five mortality rate) groups of countries are the median values for each group. The median is the middle value of a data set arranged in order of magnitude. The median is the average commonly used where there are a large number of items of data with a great range, as is the case in these tables, and it has the advantage of not being distorted by the very small or the very large countries. In cases where the range of the data is not all that extensive, the most commonly used average is the mean, which is the sum of all the values divided by the number of the items. However, because we are dealing here with countries of very different sizes of population, we would immediately encounter the problem of weighting, if we used the mean. Hence the choice of the median to give the reader some idea of the situation in a typical country of the appropriate U5MR group.

..	Data not available.
*	UNICEF field office source.
(.)	Less than half the unit shown.
T	Total (as opposed to a median).
X	See footnote at the end of the tables.
Y	UNICEF field office source; see footnote at the end of the tables.

Most of the U5MR figures are interpolations based on five-year estimates prepared by the UN Population Division on an internationally comparable basis using various sources. In some cases, these interpolated estimates may differ from the latest national figures.

Index to countries

In the following tables, countries are ranked in descending order of their estimated 1986 under-five mortality rate which has then been rounded to the nearest whole number. The reference numbers indicating that rank are given in the alphabetical list of countries below.

TABLE 1: BASIC INDICATORS

		Under 5 mortality rate		Infant mortality rate (under 1)		Total population (millions)	Annual no. of births/infant and child deaths (0–4) (thousands)	GNP per capita (US $)	Life expectancy at birth (years)	% adults literate male/female	% of age group enrolled in primary school male/female	% share of household income 1975–85	
		1960	1986	1960	1986	1986	1986	1985	1986	1985	1983–86	lowest 40%	highest 20%
	Very high U5MR countries (over 170) Median	308	**211**	185	130	477T	22519T/4730T	280	47	43/22	71/48	..	..
1	Afghanistan	380	**325**	215	185	17.2	863/280	..	39	39/8	24/11	..	..
2	Mali	370	**297**	210	171	8.3	421/125	150	44	23/11	29/17	..	..
3	Sierra Leone	397	**297**	225	171	3.7	174/52	350	36	38/21	68ˣ/48ˣ	..	..
4	Malawi	364	**270**	206	153	7.2	384/104	170	47	52/31	71/53	..	..
5	Ethiopia	294	**255**	175	151	44.7	2228/568	110	42	../..	44/28	..	..
6	Guinea	346	**255**	208	150	6.2	292/74	320	42	40/17	42/19	..	..
7	Somalia	294	**255**	175	151	4.8	226/58	280	42	18/6	32/18	..	..
8	Mozambique	302	**..**	174	..	14.3	651/161	160	47	55/22	94/74	..	..
9	Burkina Faso	388	**241**	220	141	7.1	342/82	150	47	21/6	41/24	..	..
10	Angola	346	**..**	208	..	9.0	427/101	470ˣ	44	49/..	146ˣ/121ˣ	..	..
11	Niger	320	**233**	191	137	6.3	324/76	250	44	19/9	37/20	..	..
12	Chad	326	**228**	195	134	5.1	228/52	80ˣ	45	40/11	55/21	..	..
13	Guinea-Bissau	315	**228**	188	134	0.9	37/8	180	45	46/17	81/40	..	..
14	Central African Rep.	308	**228**	183	134	2.6	117/27	260	45	53/29	98ˣ/51ˣ	..	..
15	Senegal	313	**227**	180	134	6.6	309/70	370	45	37/19	66/45	..	..
16	Mauritania	310	**225**	185	129	1.9	98/22	420	46	../..	45ˣ/29ˣ	..	..
17	Liberia	303	**211**	180	124	2.3	110/23	470	51	47/23	82*/50*	..	..
18	Rwanda	248	**210**	146	124	6.3	323/68	280	48	61/33	66/63	..	..
19	Kampuchea	218	**206**	146	132	7.5	318/66	..	48	85*/65*	100*/80*	..	..
20	Yemen	378	**204**	214	123	7.0	339/69	550	50	27/3	112/22	..	..
21	Yemen, Dem.	378	**204**	214	123	2.2	104/21	530	50	59/35	96/35	..	..
22	Bhutan	297	**202**	186	130	1.4	54/11	160	48	../..	32/18	..	..
23	Nepal	297	**202**	186	130	16.9	677/137	160	48	39/12	80*/44*	..	..
24	Burundi	258	**196**	152	116	4.9	225/44	230	48	43ˣ/26ˣ	61/44	..	..
25	Bangladesh	262	**193**	156	121	103.9	4428/854	150	49	43/22	70/50	17	45
26	Benin	310	**189**	185	112	4.2	213/40	260	46	37/16	87/43	..	..
27	Sudan	293	**182**	170	108	22.2	996/181	300	50	33ʸ/14ʸ	57*/49*	..	..
28	Tanzania, U. Rep. of	248	**179**	146	107	23.3	1184/212	290	53	93ʸ/88ʸ	79*/81*	..	..
29	Bolivia	282	**179**	167	113	6.5	284/51	470	53	84/65	96/85	..	..
30	Nigeria	318	**178**	190	107	98.5	5015/895	800	50	54/31	103/81	..	..
31	Haiti	294	**176**	197	119	6.8	278/49	310	54	40/35	83/72	6*	48*
32	Gabon	288	**174**	171	105	1.2	43/7	3670	51	70/53	124/121	..	..
33	Uganda	224	**174**	133	105	16.0	810/141	230	51	70/45	66ˣ/50ˣ	..	..
	High U5MR countries (95–170) Median	251	125	156	85	1520T	49840T/7047T	770	57	68/50	105/92	..	..
34	Pakistan	277	**170**	163	111	102.9	4211/716	380	52	40/19	66*/33*	18*	57*
35	Zaire	251	**166**	148	100	30.9	1394/232	170	52	79/45	112/84	..	..
36	Lao People's Dem. Rep.	232	**166**	155	113	4.2	165/27	..	52	92/76	101/79	..	..
37	Oman	378	**166**	214	104	1.3	58/10	6730	55	47ʸ/12ʸ	97/80	..	..
38	Iran (Islamic Rep. of)	254	**..**	169	..	45.9	1801/286	..	59	62/39	122/101	..	..
39	Cameroon	275	**158**	163	96	10.2	435/69	810	53	68/55	116/97	..	..
40	Togo	305	**157**	182	95	3.1	138/22	230	52	53/28	118/73	..	..
41	India	282	**154**	165	101	772.7	22477/3455	270	57	57/29	107/76	16	49
42	Côte d'Ivoire	320	**153**	200	102	10.2	463/71	660	52	53/31	92/65	9	61
43	Ghana	224	**150**	132	91	14.0	663/99	380	54	64/43	75/59	..	..
44	Lesotho	208	**140**	149	102	1.6	65/9	470	51	62/84	102/127	..	61
45	Zambia	228	**132**	135	82	6.9	333/44	390	53	84/67	106/96	11	61
46	Egypt	300	**131**	179	88	48.0	1629/214	610	60	59/30	94/76	17ˣ	48ˣ
47	Peru	233	**128**	142	91	20.2	708/91	1010	61	91/78	125/120	7ˣ	61ˣ
48	Libyan Arab Jamahiriya	268	**125**	160	85	3.7	167/21	7170	60	81/50	../..	..	..
49	Morocco	265	**125**	163	85	22.5	755/95	560	60	45/22	98/63	..	..
50	Indonesia	235	**122**	139	76	169.5	5020/614	530	56	83/65	121/116	14	49
51	Congo	241	**119**	143	75	1.8	80/10	1110	48	71/55	../..	..	..
52	Kenya	208	**118**	124	74	21.5	1182/139	290	55	70/49	97/91	9	60
53	Zimbabwe	182	**118**	110	74	9.1	431/51	680	57	81/67	132/126	..	..
54	Honduras	232	**112**	144	71	4.5	184/21	720	62	61/58	103/102	..	..
55	Algeria	270	**112**	168	76	22.4	938/105	2550	62	63/37	104/83	..	..
56	Tunisia	255	**106**	159	74	7.2	226/24	1190	62	68/41	127/108	..	..
57	Guatemala	230	**105**	125	61	8.2	340/36	1250	61	63/47	../..	..	..
58	Saudi Arabia	292	**105**	170	74	12.0	495/52	8850	63	35ˣ/12ˣ	77/61	..	..
59	South Africa	192	**101**	135	75	33.2	1272/128	2010	55	../..	../..	..	..
60	Nicaragua	210	**100**	140	64	3.4	145/14	770	63	../..	../..	..	..
61	Turkey	258	**99**	190	79	50.3	1486/147	1080	64	86ˣ/62ˣ	119/112	12ˣ	57ˣ
62	Iraq	222	**98**	139	71	16.4	689/67	3020ˣ	64	90/87	108/92	..	..
63	Botswana	174	**96**	119	69	1.1	57/5	840	56	73/69	98/109	..	..
64	Viet Nam	233	**95**	156	68	60.9	1835/175	..	61	88*/80*	107/94	..	..

Note: nations are listed in descending order of their 1986 under-five mortality rates (shown in bold type)

		Under 5 mortality rate		Infant mortality rate (under 1)		Total population (millions) 1986	Annual no. of births/infant and child deaths (0-4) (thousands) 1986	GNP per capita (US $) 1985	Life expectancy at birth (years) 1986	% adults literate male/female 1985	% of age group enrolled in primary school male/female 1983-86	% share of household income 1975-85	
		1960	1986	1960	1986							lowest 40%	highest 20%
	Middle U5MR countries (26–94) **Median**	138	108	92	41	2009T	43780T/2345T	1440	68	89/85	105/102	14	54
65	Madagascar	181	**94**	109	61	10.3	458/43	240	51	74/62	125/118	..	..
66	Ecuador	183	**90**	124	64	9.6	347/31	1160	65	85/80	117/117	..	..
67	Papua New Guinea	247	**90**	165	64	3.6	132/12	680	54	55/35	68/55	..	..
68	Brazil	160	**89**	116	65	138.5	4039/359	1640	65	79/76	108/99	7ˣ	67ˣ
69	Burma	229	**89**	153	64	37.9	1192/106	190	60	../..	../..	..	..
70	El Salvador	206	**88**	142	61	5.7	222/20	820	67	75/69	../..	16	47
71	Dominican Rep.	200	**86**	125	67	6.4	201/17	790	64	78/77	../..	..	..
72	Philippines	135	**75**	80	46	55.8	1757/132	580	63	86/85	105/106	14	53
73	Mexico	140	**71**	92	48	81.0	2587/183	2080	67	92/88	116/114	10	58
74	Colombia	148	**70**	93	47	29.3	693/49	1320	65	89/87	116/119	..	..
75	Syrian Arab Rep.	218	**68**	135	50	10.9	502/34	1570	65	76/43	116/101	..	..
76	Paraguay	134	**63**	86	42	3.8	132/8	860	66	91/85	104/98	..	..
77	Mongolia	158	**62**	109	46	2.0	69/4	..	64	93ˣ/86ˣ	104/106	..	..
78	Jordan	218	**62**	135	46	3.7	170/10	1560	66	87/63	98/99	..	..
79	Lebanon	92	**53**	68	41	2.7	80/4	..	67	86/69	105/95	..	..
80	Thailand	149	**53**	103	41	52.3	1290/68	800	64	94/88	93*/93*	15	50
81	Albania	164	**50**	122	41	3.1	84/4	..	72	../..	99/95	..	..
82	China	202	**47**	150	34	1072.2	19914/942	310	69	82/56	132/114	..	..
83	Sri Lanka	113	**46**	70	34	16.5	417/19	380	70	91/83	105/102	16	50
84	Venezuela	114	**44**	81	36	17.8	558/25	3080	70	88/85	109/108	10ˣ	54ˣ
85	United Arab Emirates	239	**41**	145	33	1.4	35/1	19270	69	58ˣ/38ˣ	99/99	..	..
86	Guyana	94	**39**	69	31	1.0	26/1	500	70	97/95	../..	..	..
87	Argentina	75	**39**	61	33	31.0	733/29	2130	70	96/95	107/108	14ˣ	50ˣ
88	Malaysia	106	**37**	73	27	15.9	448/16	2000	68	81/66	100/99	11ˣ	56ˣ
89	Panama	105	**34**	69	23	2.2	60/2	2100	72	89/88	107/102	7ˣ	62ˣ
90	Korea, Dem. Rep. of	120	**33**	85	25	20.9	615/21	..	69	../..	../..	..	..
91	Korea, Rep. of	120	**33**	85	25	42.0	975/33	2150	69	96ˣ/88ˣ	94/94	17	45
92	Uruguay	56	**31**	50	27	3.0	58/2	1650	71	93ˣ/94ˣ	111/109	..	..
93	Mauritius	104	**30**	70	24	1.1	26/1	1090	68	89/77	105/106	12	61
94	Romania	82	**30**	69	24	23.2	396/12	2560ˣ	71	../..	98/97	..	..
95	Yugoslavia	113	**30**	92	27	23.3	362/11	2070	72	97/86	96/96	19	39
96	USSR	53	**28**	38	23	281.3	5207/147	4550ˣ	72	../..	../..	..	..
	Low U5MR countries (25 and under) **Median**	43	13	36	10	891T	12792T/166T	7300	74	97/93	102/101	18	40
97	Chile	142	**25**	114	20	12.2	272/7	1430	71	97ʸ/96ʸ	108/106	10*	61*
98	Trinidad and Tobago	67	**25**	54	21	1.2	30/1	6020	70	97/95	93/96	13	50
99	Jamaica	88	**24**	62	19	2.3	63/2	940	74	90ˣ/93ˣ	106/107	..	..
100	Kuwait	128	**24**	89	20	1.9	68/2	14480	73	76/63	102/99	..	..
101	Costa Rica	121	**23**	84	18	2.7	78/2	1300	74	94/93	101/100	12ˣ	55ˣ
102	Portugal	112	**21**	81	18	10.3	172/4	1970	73	89/80	120/119	15ˣ	49ˣ
103	Bulgaria	62	**20**	44	15	9.1	138/3	4150ˣ	72	../..	102/101	..	..
104	Hungary	57	**20**	51	18	10.7	132/3	1950	71	../..	98/99	21	36
105	Poland	70	**20**	62	18	37.5	637/13	2050	72	../..	102/100	..	..
106	Cuba	87	**19**	62	15	10.1	181/3	..	74	96ˣ/96ˣ	108/101	..	..
107	Greece	64	**17**	53	12	9.9	145/2	3550	75	97/88	106/106	..	..
108	Czechoslovakia	32	**17**	26	14	15.6	232/4	5820ˣ	72	../..	97/98	..	..
109	Israel	40	**16**	33	14	4.3	94/2	4990	75	97/93	98/101	18	40
110	New Zealand	27	**13**	23	11	3.3	60/1	7010	74	../..	107/106	16	45
111	USA	30	**13**	26	10	240.1	3789/48	16690	75	../..	101/101	17	40
112	Austria	43	**13**	37	10	7.5	93/1	9120	74	../..	100/98	..	..
113	Belgium	35	**13**	31	9	9.9	122/2	8280	74	../..	94/96	22	36
114	German Dem. Rep.	44	**13**	37	9	16.8	240/3	7180ˣ	73	../..	102/100	..	..
115	Italy	50	**13**	44	11	57.3	658/8	6520	75	98/96	99/99	18	44
116	Singapore	50	**12**	36	9	2.6	43/1	7420	73	93/79	118/113	..	..
117	Germany, Fed. Rep. of	38	**12**	31	9	60.7	636/7	10940	74	../..	96/96	20	40
118	Ireland	36	**12**	31	9	3.7	79/1	4850	74	../..	100/100	20ˣ	39ˣ
119	Spain	56	**11**	46	9	38.8	580/7	4290	75	97/92	108/107	19	40
120	United Kingdom	27	**11**	23	9	56.1	743/8	8460	74	../..	103/103	19	40
121	Australia	25	**11**	21	10	15.9	249/3	10830	76	../..	106/105	15	47
122	Hong Kong	65	**11**	44	9	5.6	94/1	6230	76	95/81	106/104	16	47
123	France	34	**10**	29	8	54.8	765/8	9540	75	../..	108/106	17	42
124	Canada	33	**10**	28	8	25.7	384/4	13680	76	../..	106/104	17	40
125	Denmark	25	**9**	22	7	4.1	56/1	11200	75	../..	98/99	17	39
126	Japan	40	**9**	31	6	121.4	1522/14	11300	77	../..	101/102	22	38
127	Netherlands	22	**9**	18	8	14.6	173/2	9290	76	../..	94/96	22	36
128	Switzerland	27	**9**	22	7	6.4	70/1	16370	77	../..	../..	20	38
129	Norway	23	**8**	19	7	4.2	49/0	14370	76	../..	97/97	19	38
130	Finland	28	**7**	22	6	4.9	63/0	10890	75	../..	104/103	18	38
131	Sweden	20	**7**	16	6	8.3	87/1	11890	77	../..	97/99	21	42

65

TABLE 2: NUTRITION

		% of infants with low birth-weight 1982–85	% of mothers breast-feeding 1980–86			% of children under five suffering from mild-moderate/severe malnutrition 1980–86	Prevalence of wasting aged 12–23 months (% of age group) 1980–86	Average index of food production per capita (1979–81=100) 1983–85	Daily per capita calorie supply as % of requirements 1985
			3 months	6 months	12 months				
	Very high U5MR countries (over 170) Median	15	95	90	70	31/7	21	106	92
1	Afghanistan	17*	20*	6*	5*	20*/..	..	104	92
2	Mali	13	..	..	..	../..	26	114	69
3	Sierra Leone	14	98*	94y	83y	24*/3*	36*	108	85
4	Malawi	10	..	..	96*	30*/..	28	105	95
5	Ethiopia	13	..	97y	95y	60*/10*	36*	97	94
6	Guinea	18	100*	70*	40*		..	102	85
7	Somalia	..	92y	78y	54y	16y/..	..	102	91
8	Mozambique	15*	..	..	..	../..		98	68
9	Burkina Faso	21	..	..	..	../..	17x	114	87
10	Angola	19	96x	..	..	../..	..	102	86
11	Niger	20	90*	80*	60*	17*/9*	21	96	97
12	Chad	11	..	..	..	../..		106	79
13	Guinea-Bissau	15	100*	100*	98*	../..		..	105
14	Central African Rep.	23	..	..	..	../..		105	92
15	Senegal	10	94	94	82	20/..	20	105	109
16	Mauritania	10				30*/10*		94	97
17	Liberia	..	96*	92*	70*	31*/4*	7	114	103
18	Rwanda	17	80*	24*	9*	29*/8*	23	106	87
19	Kampuchea	..	100*	93*	79*	32*/5*	..	153	85
20	Yemen	9	80x	76x	55x	54x/4x	17x	112	93
21	Yemen, Dem.	12	80*	60*	55*	32*/8*	36x	100	93
22	Bhutan	..				33/6	..	110	
23	Nepal	..	99x	99x	97x	50y/7y	27x	116	88
24	Burundi	14	..	95*	90*	30/5	36	106	99
25	Bangladesh	50	98*	97x	89x	63*/21*	21	110	78
26	Benin	10	95*	90*	75*	../..	14	121	94
27	Sudan	15	91x	86x	72x	33*/8*		103	93
28	Tanzania, U. Rep. of	14	100*	90*	70*	43*/7*	17*	108	99
29	Bolivia	13*	93x	91x	48x	49y/3y	..	101	88
30	Nigeria	25	98*	80*	60*	24/..	16*	109	92
31	Haiti	17	90*	71y	29y	65*/5*	18y	104	79
32	Gabon	16	..	..	..	../..		..	124
33	Uganda	10	85*	70*	20*	15y/4y		125	109
	High U5MR countries (95–170) Median	13	95	90	71	33/5	14	109	100
34	Pakistan	27	78*	73*	67*	60*/10*	14	114	93
35	Zaire	20*	100x	100x	85x	15*/5*	..	113	96
36	Lao People's Dem. Rep.	15	..	..	..	38*/..	..	129	96
37	Oman	14	..	..	..	../..	..	..	..
38	Iran (Islamic Rep. of)	10*	..	..	..	../..	..	109	118
39	Cameroon	13	..	98x	97x	../..	..	107	89
40	Togo	20*	..	99x	90x	../..	9x	103	97
41	India	30	..	..	..	33*/5*	37	120	94
42	Côte d'Ivoire	14	93*	90*	50*	../..	21*	115	102
43	Ghana	17*	100*	70*	25*	23*/7*	28	118	78
44	Lesotho	10	..	87*	..	../..	7	93	100
45	Zambia	..	..	..	93*	../..	..	107	85
46	Egypt	7	..	91y	84y	46y/..	..	115	127
47	Peru	9	80*	67*	37*	38*/..	..	111	84
48	Libyan Arab Jamahiriya	5	..	..	..	../..	..	..	152
49	Morocco	9	95*	61*	..	40y/5y	..	113	108
50	Indonesia	14	98*	97*	83*	27*/3*	17	117	109
51	Congo	15	97*	97*	85*	30x/..		104	108
52	Kenya	13	89*	84x	44x	30*/2*	8x	99	87
53	Zimbabwe	15	98*	95*	84*	../..	..	100	84
54	Honduras	9	48*	28*	24*	29*/2*	..	104	95
55	Algeria	9*	..	..	..	../..	108	121	..
56	Tunisia	7	95*	92*	71*	60y/4y	..	114	119
57	Guatemala	18	..	84x	74x	../..	..	108	99
58	Saudi Arabia	6	..	91*	52*	../..	9	..	132
59	South Africa	12	..	..	..	../..	..	88	118
60	Nicaragua	15	..	..	71*	../..	..	90	105
61	Turkey	7	99*	91*	51*	../..	..	108	125
62	Iraq	9	..	..	..	../..		114	118
63	Botswana	8*	97*	90*	75*	31*/..	19*	96	95
64	Viet Nam	18*	93*	88*	20*	39*/13*	12*	122	97

Note: nations are listed in descending order of their 1986 under-five mortality rates (see table 1)

	% of infants with low birth-weight 1982–85	% of mothers breast-feeding 1980–86			% of children under five suffering from mild-moderate/severe malnutrition 1980–86	Prevalence of wasting aged 12–23 months (% of age group) 1980–86	Average index of food production per capita (1979–81=100) 1983–85	Daily per capita calorie supply as % of requirements 1985
		3 months	6 months	12 months				
Middle U5MR countries (26–94) **Median**	9	67	52	30	40/..	..	110	113
65 Madagascar	11	95*	95*	85*	../..	..	112	111
66 Ecuador	..	..	..	57*	40^y/..	..	104	88
67 Papua New Guinea	25	..	..	..	38^y/..	..	109	79
68 Brazil	8*	59*	19*	5*	55^y/..	..	115	107
69 Burma	20	90*	90*	90*	50^y/..	48	129	117
70 El Salvador	13	..	77	55	52*/6*	..	100	91
71 Dominican Rep.	15	65*	50*	25*	39^y/2^y	..	113	110
72 Philippines	18*	68^x	58^x	28^x	18*/4*	14*	103	101
73 Mexico	15	62^x	48^x	27^x	../..	..	110	126
74 Colombia	10	84*	58*	28*	43*/8*	10	103	111
75 Syrian Arab Rep.	9	88^x	72^x	41^x	23*/2*	..	108	129
76 Paraguay	6	80^x	77^x	49^x	../..	..	111	127
77 Mongolia	10	..	..	..	../..	..	111	117
78 Jordan	7	70*	52*	25*	../..	9^x	121	117
79 Lebanon	10	50*	40*	15*	../..	..	112	101
80 Thailand	12	48^x	47^x	20^x	27*/(.)*	18^x	119	102
81 Albania	7	..	..	..	../..	..	109	118
82 China	6	..	..	..	../..	..	125	111
83 Sri Lanka	25	83^x	74^x	48^x	../..	22^x	98	114
84 Venezuela	9	50^x	40^x	30^x	../..	..	101	95
85 United Arab Emirates	7	..	..	..	../..	..	..	..
86 Guyana	20*	77	60	35	54*/..	..		122
87 Argentina	6	..	..	..	../..	..	106	122
88 Malaysia	10	47^x	34^x	19^x	../..	6	116	110
89 Panama	8	62^x	48^x	30^x	48^y/3^y	8	109	98
90 Korea, Dem. Rep. of	..	..	..	..	../..	..	116	126
91 Korea, Rep. of	9	94^x	93^x	84^x	../..	..	109	117
92 Uruguay	8*	51*	21*	13*	../..	..	107	103
93 Mauritius	9	59*	49*	38*	17*/7*	20*	105	118
94 Romania	6	..	..	..	../..	..	110	127
95 Yugoslavia	7	..	..	..	../..	..	102	134
96 USSR	6	..	..	..	../..	..	110	128
Low U5MR countries (25 and under) **Median**	6	..	..	..	../..	..	108	128
97 Chile	6*	..	..	..	9*/(.)*	11	103	102
98 Trinidad and Tobago	..	59^x	50^x	14^x	48*/..	..	95	126
99 Jamaica	8*	57^x	40^x	16^x	39*/1	14*	109	112
100 Kuwait	7	..	..	..	../..	3	..	..
101 Costa Rica	9	38^x	20^x	9^x	46^y/..	..	100	118
102 Portugal	8	..	..	..	../..	..	100	124
103 Bulgaria	6	..	..	..	../..	..	101	146
104 Hungary	10	45^x	21^x	4^x	../..	..	111	135
105 Poland	8	42^x	32^x	..	../..	..	106	126
106 Cuba	9	..	..	..	../..	..	110	127
107 Greece	6	..	..	..	../..	..	104	145
108 Czechoslovakia	6	..	..	..	../..	..	118	143
109 Israel	7	..	..	..	../..	..	117	119
110 New Zealand	5	..	..	..	../..	..	110	131
111 USA	7	33	25	8	../..	..	100	140
112 Austria	6	..	..	..	../..	..	108	130
113 Belgium	5	..	..	..	../..	..	98	139
114 German Dem. Rep.	6	..	..	..	../..	..	105	143
115 Italy	7	..	..	..	../..	..	103	143
116 Singapore	8	..	..	..	../..	9	98	114
117 Germany, Fed. Rep. of	5	..	..	..	../..	..	110	133
118 Ireland	4	..	..	..	../..	..	108	140
119 Spain	..	..	..	..	../..	..	104	130
120 United Kingdom	7	..	..	..	../..	..	109	129
121 Australia	6	..	..	..	../..	..	110	114
122 Hong Kong	8	..	18^x	..	../..	..	108	119
123 France	5	..	..	..	../..	..	107	142
124 Canada	6	26^x	13^x	..	../..	..	110	130
125 Denmark	6	..	..	..	../..	..	118	129
126 Japan	5	..	..	..	../..	..	106	106
127 Netherlands	4	17^x	..	..	../..	..	107	128
128 Switzerland	5	..	..	..	../..	..	108	126
129 Norway	4	..	..	..	../..	..	109	114
130 Finland	4	..	..	..	../..	..	114	111
131 Sweden	4	..	..	..	../..	..	108	114

TABLE 3: HEALTH

| | | % of population with access to drinking water 1983–86 | % of population with access to health services 1980–86 | Percentage fully immunized 1981/1985–86 | | | | | ORS per 100 episodes of Diarrhoea (litres) 1985 | % of births attended by trained health personnel 1984 | Maternal mortality rate 1980–84 |
| | | | | One-year-old children | | | | Pregnant women Tetanus | | | |
		Total/urban/rural	Total/urban/rural	TB	DPT	Polio	Measles				
	Very high U5MR countries (over 170) Median	29/ 61 /21	40/ 80 /30	27/46	14/20	8/21	19/39	5/12	20	22	450
1	Afghanistan	16*/ 56*/10*	29*/ 80*/17*	8/16	3/9	3/9	6/12	3/10	37	. .	640x
2	Mali	12*/ 23*/ 9*	15/ . . /. .	19/15*	. ./3*	. ./3*	. ./5*	1/3*	8	. .	
3	Sierra Leone	22/ 61 / 6	. ./ . /. .	35/80x	15/21x	13/21x	28/66x	10/17x	57	25	450
4	Malawi	51/ 66 /49	80/ . . /. .	86/79	66/54	68/55	65/42	. ./47*	9	59	250x
5	Ethiopia*	6*/ . . /. .	46*/ . . /. .	10/12y	6/6y	7/6y	7/9y	. ./6*	38	58	
6	Guinea	17/ 69 / 2	. ./ . . /. .	4*/46*	. ./10*	. ./8*	15*/41*	5*/17*	2	. .	
7	Somalia	36/ 65 /21	27*/ 50*/15*	3/29	2/18	2/18	3/26	5/7	27	2	1100
8	Mozambique	13y/ 50y/ 7y	30*/ . . /. .	46/45*	56/32*	32/32*	32/39*	. ./59*	10	28	300x
9	Burkina Faso	30/ 27 /31	49*/ 51*/48*	16/67	2/36	2/36	23/68	11/1*	8	. .	1500x
10	Angola	28/ 90 /12	30/ . . /. .	. ./59*	. ./20*	. ./58*	. ./44*	. ./54*	17	15	
11	Niger	34/ 41 /33	40*/ 99*/30*	28/27y	6/4y	6/23y	19/49y	3/16*	2	47	420
12	Chad	26x/ . . /. .	. ./ . /. .	. ./15	. ./3	. ./3	. ./7	. ./3	28	. .	
13	Guinea-Bissau	33/ 21 /37	. ./ . /. .	. ./47*	. ./11*	. ./11*	. ./34*	. ./16*	19	. .	400
14	Central African Rep.	16x/ . . /. .	. ./ . /. .	26/59y	12/24y	12/24y	16/30y	13/20*	23	. .	600
15	Senegal	42/ 69 /27	. ./ . /. .	. ./32	. ./54	. ./54	. ./54	. ./40	10	. .	530x
16	Mauritania	. ./ 80 /. .	30*/ . . /. .	57/74y	18/21y	18/21y	45/59y	1/. .	2	23	
17	Liberia	20*/ . . /. .	28*/ 40*/20*	87/50*	39/25*	26/25*	. ./50*	. ./16*	5	89	
18	Rwanda	59/ 55 /60	27*/ 60*/25*	51/86*	17/67*	15/72*	42/55*	5/26*	24	. .	210
19	Kampuchea	. ./ . . /. .	55*/ 80*/50*	. ./54*	. ./37*	. ./35*	. ./54*	. ./3*	91	. .	
20	Yemen	31*/ 99*/21*	30*/ 75*/24*	15/28	25/16	25/16	40/19	. ./3	20	12	
21	Yemen, Dem.	53*/ 79*/39*	30*/ . . /. .	9/12	5/6	5/5	6/6	3/5	105	10	100
22	Bhutan	15/ 40 /14	19/ . . /. .	36/32	8/16	7/16	9/15	. ./4	21	3	
23	Nepal	15/ 71 /11	. ./ . /. .	32/67	16/38	1/34	2/66	4/13	14	10	850x
24	Burundi	39/ 94 /22	45*/ 90*/30*	65/80	38/60	6/61	30/57	25/17	26	12	600
25	Bangladesh	41/ 29 /43	45*/ . . /. .	1/5	1/5	1/4	(.)/ 3	1/5	18	. .	600
26	Benin	18/ 26 /15	40*/ . . /. .	. ./44*	. ./19*	. ./19*	. ./22*	. ./82x	12	34	1680x
27	Sudan	25/ 60 /10	55/ 90 /40	3/23	1/14	1/14	1/11	1/6	87	20	
28	Tanzania, U. Rep. of	50/ 88 /39	76*/ 99y /72y	78/82*	58/62*	49/62*	76/67*	36/58*	36	74	370x
29	Bolivia	43/ 77 /12	23*/ . . /. .	30/15*	13/38*	15/31*	17x/65*	. ./1	97	. .	480x
30	Nigeria	33/ 58 /25	40*/ 75*/30*	23/30	24*/14	24*/14	55/16	11/11	2	. .	1500
31	Haiti	32*/ 50*/25*	55*/ . . /. .	60/57	14/19	3/19	. ./21	. ./56*	7	20	156
32	Gabon	. ./ . . /. .	. ./ . /. .	. ./79y	. ./48y	. ./48y	. ./55y	. ./32	27	. .	124
33	Uganda	16*/ 90*/ 7*	61*/ 90*/57*	18/51*	9/21*	8/21*	22/33*	20/5*	21	. .	300
	High U5MR countries (95–170) Median	51/ 73 /33	74/ 99 /62	55/73	35/54	37/58	26/51	8/22	22	60	145
34	Pakistan	47*/ 83*/38*	55*/ 99*/35*	11/68	3/55	3/55	2/40	1/28	28	24	600
35	Zaire	17*/ 35*/ 5*	25*/ . . /. .	34/45*	18/30*	18/30*	17/30*	. ./35*	4	. .	800
36	Lao People's Dem. Rep.	21/ 28 /20	. ./ . /. .	4/11*	7*/ 8*	7*/ 8*	7*/ 4*	2*/ 8*	34	. .	
37	Oman	14y/ 70y/10y	91*/100*/90*	49/90*	9/84*	9/84*	6/76*	27/70*	82	60	
38	Iran (Islamic Rep. of)	76*/ 95*/55*	71*/ 95*/45*	6/75	29/69	47/72	48/73	2/28	11	. .	
39	Cameroon	26x/ . . /. .	. ./ . . /. .	8/83*	5/45*	5/42*	16/44*	. ./17*	1	. .	141x
40	Togo	35/ 68 /26	61*/ . . /. .	44/66y	9/41y	9/40y	47/48y	57/64*	21	. .	84x
41	India	54/ 80 /47	. ./ . . /. .	12/29	31/53	7/45	. ./1	24/40	5	33	500
42	Côte d'Ivoire	18/ 30 /10	32*/ 61*/11*	70/16y	42/11y	34/11y	28/31y	25/32y	17	. .	
43	Ghana	50/ 72 /47	60*/ 92*/45*	67/37y	22/14y	25/13y	23/45y	11/8*	26	73	1074x
44	Lesotho	14/ 37 /11	. ./ . /. .	81/91y	56/82y	54/80y	49/73y	0*/ 0*	41	28	
45	Zambia	47/ 65 /33	75*/ . . /. .	72*/82*	44*/46*	77*/46*	21*/55*	. ./38*	42	. .	109
46	Egypt	75/ 88 /64	. ./ . /. .	71/84	82/87	84/86	65/85	10/8	21	24	80
47	Peru	55/ 73 /18	. ./ . /17*	63/53*	18/50*	18/50*	24x/41*	4/6*	15	44	314
48	Libyan Arab Jamahiriya	96/100 /90	. ./ . /. .	55/77	55/62	55/62	57/50	6/12	. .	76	80x
49	Morocco	30*/ 63*/ 2*	73*/100*/50*	. ./71	43/53	45/53	. ./48	. ./. .	18	. .	327
50	Indonesia	36*/ 53*/30*	75*/ . . /. .	55/67	(.)/48	(.)/46	(.)/47	10/26	22	43*	800
51	Congo	21/ 42 /7	. ./ . /. .	92/91*	42/65*	42/71y	49/86*	. ./11*	23	. .	
52	Kenya	28/ 61 /21	. ./ . /. .	. ./80	. ./72	. ./72	. ./65	. ./40	10	. .	168x
53	Zimbabwe	52y/ . . /. .	71*/100*/62*	64/76*	39/63*	38/63*	56/53*	. ./40*	4	69	145x
54	Honduras	69/ 91 /55	73/ 85 /65	46/67*	38/62*	37/62*	38x/55*	11/18	120	50	82x
55	Algeria	89*/100*/80*	89/100 /80	59/88y	33/68y	30/68y	17/67y	. ./. .	22	. .	129
56	Tunisia	75*/100*/50*	90*/100*/80*	65/80	36/70	37/70	65/65	2/11	106	60	
57	Guatemala	51/ 90 /26	34*/ 47*/25*	29/30	42x/31*	42x/32*	8/42	1/2*	11	. .	105
58	Saudi Arabia	91/100 /68	97*/100*/88*	49/88y	53/84y	52/84y	12/79y	. ./. .	48	78	
59	South Africa	. ./ . /. .	. ./ . /. .	. ./. .						. .	65x
60	Nicaragua	56/ 91 / 10	83*/100*/60*	65/95*	23/45*	52/80*	20/51*	. ./25*	92	. .	
61	Turkey	63y/ 63y/63y	. ./ . /. .	42/24*	64/45	69/45	52/36	. ./4*	3	78y	207x
62	Iraq	89*/100*/46*	93*/ 97*/78*	76/78*	13/91*	16/91*	33/75*	4/43*	39	60	
63	Botswana	65/ 98 / 47	89*/100*/85*	80/67	64/64	71/60	68/62	32/16	38	52y	300
64	Viet Nam	41*/ 60*/32*	80*/100*/75*	. ./57	. ./43	. ./44	. ./37	. ./. .	10	99	110

Note: nations are listed in descending order of their 1986 under-five mortality rates (see table 1)

		% of population with access to drinking water 1983-86	% of population with access to health services 1980-86	Percentage fully immunized 1981/1985-86					ORS per 100 episodes of Diarrhoea (litres) 1985	% of births attended by trained health personnel 1984	Maternal mortality 1980-84
		Total/urban/rural	Total/urban/rural	One-year-old children				Pregnant women Tetanus			
				TB	DPT	Polio	Measles				
	Middle U5MR countries (26–94) Median	66/ 86 /42	78/ . . /. .	58/77	47/66	48/71	42/55	12/44	21	82	90
65	Madagascar	23/ 73 /9	60*/ . . /. .	25/10	40/30	8/30	. ./10	. ./18	34	62	300x
66	Ecuador	61/ 98 /21	18*/ . . /. .	82/93*	26/44*	19/44*	31x/50*	4/11y		27	220x
67	Papua New Guinea	16/ 55 /10	. ./ . . /. .	64/78	31/43	31/37	. ./29	. ./. .	20	34	1000
68	Brazil	76/ 86 /53	. ./ . . /. .	62/58	47/62	99x/86	73x/63	. ./. .	28	73	154
69	Burma	23/ 36 /21	50*/100*/31*	15/32	5/20	. ./4	. ./3	6/21	84	97	135
70	El Salvador	. ./ . . /42		47/50	42/70*	38x/70*	44/24*	20/19*	64	35	74
71	Dominican Rep.	60/ 85 /32	80*/ . . /. .	34/51	27/93*	42/82y	17x/89y	26/87*	152	98	56x
72	Philippines	66*/ 83*/54*	. ./ . . /. .	61/72	51x/55	44/55	. ./53	37/49	19	. .	80
73	Mexico	75/ 91 /40	45*/ . . /. .	41/16	41/40	85/92y	33x/74x	. ./. .	18	. .	92
74	Colombia	63*/ 84*/20*	75*/ . . /. .	57/77*	20/61	22/62	26/51*	6/6y	53	51	126
75	Syrian Arab Rep.	75y/ 98y/54y	75*/ 92*/60*	36/82*	14/73*	14/73*	14/70*	3/19*	6	37	280
76	Paraguay	26/ 46 /10	60*/ 90*/38*	42/99	28/54	26/97	16/46	6/61*	10	22	469
77	Mongolia			53/52	99/81	99/86	. ./10	. ./. .	20	99	140x
78	Jordan	93*/100*/80*	97*/ 98*/95*	0/2y	81/53	87/54	40/39	2/52	61	75	. .
79	Lebanon	92y/ 95y/85y	. ./ . . /. .	. ./4*	. ./30	. ./30	. ./30	. ./. .	2	45	. .
80	Thailand	66/ 50 /70	70*/ . . /. .	71/83	52/62	31/62	. ./39	27/45	34	33	270
81	Albania	. ./ . . /. .	. ./ . . /. .	93/92	94/96	92/94	90/96	. ./. .			
82	China	. ./ 85y/. .	. ./ . . /. .	. ./70y	. ./62y	. ./68y	. ./63y	. ./. .			44
83	Sri Lanka	36/ 76 /26	93*/ . . /. .	58/76	45/77	46/77	. ./47	57/44	59	87	90
84	Venezuela	. ./ . . /65		77/92x	54/49	75/59	43/56	. ./. .	58	82	65
85	United Arab Emirates	93x/ 95x/81x	90*/ . . /. .	18/88	45/72	45/73	42/66	. ./. .	23	96	
86	Guyana	73/100 /60	89*/ . . /. .	. ./76*	45/64*	37/67*	. ./42*	. ./93*	14	93	104x
87	Argentina	63/ 72 /17	70*/ 80*/21*	63/89	46/63	38/69	73/67x		13	. .	85x
88	Malaysia	69*/ 93*/53*	. ./ . . /. .	91/99*	59/68*	61/68*	. ./48*	20/48*	19	82	59
89	Panama	62/ 97 /26	80*/ 95*/64*	77/94	49/73	50/71	53/83	. ./29*	18	83	90
90	Korea, Dem. Rep. of	. ./ . . /60		52/53	52/61	51/62	31/44	. ./. .		99	41
91	Korea, Rep. of	. ./ . . /60	93*/ 97*/86*	42/47x	61/76x	62/80x	5/88x	. ./. .		. .	34
92	Uruguay	81/ 95 / 3	80*/ . ./. .	76/92*	57/70*	58/84y	95x/76x	18/13y	21	. .	56x
93	Mauritius	95*/ 95*/95*	98*/100*/97*	87/86	82/84	82/84	. ./70	1/55	12	84	52
94	Romania	. ./ . . /. .	. ./ . . /. .	. ./. .	. ./95	. ./92	. ./88	. ./. .		99	175
95	Yugoslavia	. ./ . . /. .	. ./ . . /. .	99/85	90/89	95/90	95/91	. ./. .		. .	27
96	USSR	. ./ . . /. .	. ./ . . /. .	. ./93	95/85	95/99	95/95	. ./. .		100	. .
	Low U5MR countries (25 and under) Median	. ./ . . /. .	. ./ . . /. .	92/88	84/90	90/90	69/78	. ./. .	. .	99	11
97	Chile	85/100 /18	. ./ . . /. .	93/100*	91/91*	93/85	63/91*		3	95	55
98	Trinidad and Tobago	99/100 /96	. ./ . . /. .	. ./. .	52/70*	55/71*	. ./45y	. ./60y	18	90	81x
99	Jamaica	86x/ . . /. .	. ./ . . /. .	. ./73*	39/74*	37/74*	. ./36*	50*/50*	0	89	102
100	Kuwait	89x/ . . /. .	93*/ . . /. .	. ./4*	54/90*	76/90*	66/5*	30/2*	38	99	18
101	Costa Rica	91/100 /82	80*/100*/63*	81/92*	83/90*	85/90*	71/95*	. ./90*	67	93	26
102	Portugal	. ./ . . /. .	. ./ . . /. .	74/82	75/76	16/77	70/66	. ./. .			15
103	Bulgaria	. ./ . . /. .	. ./ . . /. .	97/99	97/99	98/99	98/99	98/. .		100	22
104	Hungary	. ./ . . /. .	. ./ . . /. .	99/99x	99/99	98/99	99/99	. ./. .		99	28
105	Poland	. ./ . . /. .	. ./ . . /. .	95/95	95/96x	95/97x	65/95	. ./. .		. .	12
106	Cuba	. ./ . . /. .	. ./ . . /. .	97/98	67/91	82/88x	49/85	. ./. .		. .	31
107	Greece	. ./ . . /. .	. ./ . . /. .	95/56x	95/54	95/96	. ./77	. ./. .		. .	12
108	Czechoslovakia	. ./ . . /. .	. ./ . . /. .	95/99	95/99	95/99	95/98	. ./. .		100	8
109	Israel	. ./ . . /. .	. ./ . . /. .	70/. .	84/85	91/87	69/85	. ./. .		99	5
110	New Zealand	. ./ . . /. .	. ./ . . /. .	. ./20	72x/72	. ./83	. ./71x	. ./. .		99	20
111	USA	. ./ . . /. .	. ./ . . /. .	. ./. .	. ./37x	. ./24x	96x/82x	. ./. .		100	9
112	Austria	. ./ . . /. .	. ./ . . /. .	90/90x	90/90x	90/90x	90/25x	. ./. .			11
113	Belgium	. ./ . . /. .	. ./ . . /. .	. ./. .	95/95x	99/95x	50/. .	. ./. .		100	10
114	German Dem. Rep.	. ./ . . /. .	. ./ . . /. .	95/99	80/94	90/94	95/99	. ./. .		. .	17
115	Italy	. ./ . . /. .	. ./ . . /. .	. ./50x	. ./12	. ./90x	. ./12	. ./. .			13
116	Singapore	100/100 /. .	. ./ . . / . .	83/72	87/78	88/81	57x/73x	. ./90		100	11
117	Germany, Fed. Rep. of	. ./ . . /. .	. ./ . . /. .	40/30	50/30	80/80	35/25	. ./. .			11
118	Ireland	. ./ . . /. .	. ./ . . /. .	. ./80	36/45	76/90	. ./63	. ./. .			7
119	Spain	. ./ . . /. .	. ./ . . /. .	. ./. .	. ./87	. ./87	. ./79	. ./. .		96	10x
120	United Kingdom	. ./ . . /. .	. ./ . . /. .	. ./5x	44/60x	71/78x	52/62x	. ./. .		98	7
121	Australia	. ./ . . /. .	. ./ . . /. .	. ./. .	. ./. .	. ./. .	. ./68x	. ./. .		99	11
122	Hong Kong	99/100 /93	. ./ . . /. .	. ./99	84/87	94/92	. ./. .	. ./90		. .	6
123	France	. ./ . . /. .	. ./ . . /. .	80/96	79/97	80/97	(.)/55	. ./. .		. .	13
124	Canada	. ./ . . /. .	. ./ . . /. .	. ./. .	. ./. .	. ./. .	. ./. .	. ./. .		99	2
125	Denmark	. ./ . . /. .	. ./ . . /. .	95/85x	85/94x	97/94x	. ./. .	. ./. .			4
126	Japan	. ./ . . /. .	. ./ . . /. .	85/85x	. ./98x	. ./98x	. ./73x	. ./. .			15
127	Netherlands	. ./ . . /. .	. ./ . . /. .	. ./. .	97/97x	97/97	93/93	. ./. .			5
128	Switzerland	. ./ . . /. .	. ./ . . /. .	. ./. .	. ./. .	. ./. .	. ./. .	. ./. .			5
129	Norway	. ./ . . /. .	. ./ . . /. .	. ./90x	. ./85	. ./90	. ./90	. ./. .		100	4
130	Finland	. ./ . . /. .	. ./ . . /. .	90/90x	92/94x	90/78x	70/81x	. ./. .		100	5
131	Sweden	. ./ . . /. .	. ./ . . /. .	. ./14	99x/99x	99/98	56/92	. ./. .			4

TABLE 4: EDUCATION

		Adult literacy rate		No. of radio/ television receivers per 1,000 population 1985	Primary-school enrolment ratio			% of grade 1 enrolment completing primary school 1980-86	Secondary-school enrolment ratio 1983-86 male/female
		1970 male/female	1985 male/female		1960 (gross) male/female	1983-86 (gross) male/female	1983-86 (net) male/female		
	Very high U5MR countries (over 170) Median	**25/8**	**43/22**	**58/4**	**28/13**	**71/48**	**53/40**	**41**	**18/6**
1	Afghanistan	13/2	39/8	91/6	15/2	24/11	20/10	54*	11/5
2	Mali	11/4	23/11	16/(.)	14/6	29/17	../..	25*	10/4
3	Sierra Leone	18/8	38/21	222/8	30/15	68ˣ/48ˣ	../..	48ʸ	23ˣ/11ˣ
4	Malawi	42/18	52/31	245/..	../45	71/53	47/41	28	6/2
5	Ethiopia	8/1	../..	184/2	11/3	44/28	../..	41*	14/9
6	Guinea	21/7	40/17	30/1	44/16	42/19	33/15	37	18/6
7	Somalia	5/1	18/6	43/(.)	13/5	32/18	../..	33*	23/12
8	Mozambique	29/14	55/22	32/(.)	60/36	94/74	53/45	26	9/4
9	Burkina Faso	13/3	21/6	21/5	12/5	41/24	35/20	75	7/3
10	Angola	16/7	49/..	26/5	../..	146ˣ/121ˣ	71ˣ/61ˣ	24	../..
11	Niger	6/2	19/9	49/2	7/3	37/20	../..	67ʸ	9/3
12	Chad	20/2	40/11	219/..	29/4	55/21	../..	29ʸ	11/2
13	Guinea-Bissau	13/6	46/17	34/..	35/15	81/40	71/35	18	18/4
14	Central African Rep.	26/6	53/29	58/2	53/12	98ˣ/51ˣ	79ˣ/42ˣ	53	24ˣ/8ˣ
15	Senegal	18/5	37/19	109/31	36/17	66/45	52/36	86	18/9
16	Mauritania	../..	../..	132/(.)	13/3	45ˣ/29ˣ	../..	80	19ˣ/6ˣ
17	Liberia	27/8	47/23	228/16	45/18	82ˣ/50*	../..	..	33ˣ/13ˣ
18	Rwanda	43/21	61/33	58/..	68/30	66/63	62/60	47	3/2
19	Kampuchea	../23	85*/65*	110/7	../..	100*/80*	../..	50*	45*/20*
20	Yemen	9/1	27/3	22/4	14/..	112/22	../..	15*	17/3
21	Yemen, Dem.	31/9	59/25	70/18	20/5	96/35	../..	40*	26/11
22	Bhutan	../..	../..	14/..	5/..	32/18	../..	25ʸ	6/1
23	Nepal	23/3	39/12	30/1	19/1	80*/44*	51*/29*	27*	51*/19*
24	Burundi	29/10	43ˣ/26ˣ	53/(.)	27/9	61/44	47/35	94	5/3
25	Bangladesh	36/12	43/22	40/3	66/26	70/50	63/45	20	26/10
26	Benin	23/8	37/16	74/4	38/15	87/43	68/34	15*	29/12
27	Sudan	28/6	33ʸ/14ʸ	251/51	35/14	57*/49*	../..	61*	19*/13*
28	Tanzania, U. Rep. of	48/18	93ʸ/88ʸ	89/(.)	33/18	79*/81*	66*/68*	76	5*/3*
29	Bolivia	68/46	84/65	581/66	78/50	96/85	86/77	32ʸ	40/34
30	Nigeria	35/14	54/31	85/5	46/27	103/81	../..	31*	../..
31	Haiti	26/17	40/35	21/3	50/42	83/72	45/42	45ʸ	19/17
32	Gabon	43/22	70/53	96/19	../..	124/121	../..	59	30/20
33	Uganda	52/30	70/45	22/6	../32	66ˣ/50ˣ	43/38ˣ	58ʸ	11ˣ/5ˣ
	High U5MR countries (95–170) Median	**48/20**	**68/50**	**133/52**	**68/38**	**105/92**	**88/81**	**68**	**45/29**
34	Pakistan	30/11	40/19	90/13	46/13	66*/33*	../..	34*	21*/8*
35	Zaire	61/22	79/45	100/(.)	88/32	112/84	86/65	65ʸ	81/33
36	Lao People's Dem. Rep.	37/28	92/76	104/..	34/16	101/79	80/74	14*	23/15
37	Oman	../..	47ʸ/12ʸ	644/725	../..	97/80	80/74	60ʸ	43/21
38	Iran (Islamic Rep. of)	40/17	62/39	224/56	56/27	122/101	98/86	70ˣ	54/37
39	Cameroon	47/19	68/55	95/..	87/43	116/97	../..	70*	29/18
40	Togo	27/7	53/28	206/5	63/24	118/73	../..	43	33/10
41	India	47/20	57/29	66/5	80/40	107/76	../..	38ʸ	45/24
42	Côte d'Ivoire	26/10	53/31	133/51	68/24	92/65	../..	89ʸ	27/12
43	Ghana	43/18	64/43	184/10	52/25	75/59	../..	75ʸ	45/27
44	Lesotho	49/74	62/84	28/(.)	63/102	102/127	../..	27*	18/26
45	Zambia	66/37	84/67	30/14	51/34	106/96	88/84	85	23/13
46	Egypt	50/20	59/30	256/82	80/52	94/76	../..	64	73/52
47	Peru	81/60	91/78	203/76	95/71	125/120	../..	51*	68/61
48	Libyan Arab Jamahiriya	60/13	81/50	222/65	92/24	../..	../..	82	../..
49	Morocco	34/10	45/22	175/52	67/27	98/63	76/50	70*	38/25
50	Indonesia	66/42	83/65	117/39	86/58	121/116	100/96	80*	45/34
51	Congo	50/19	71/55	115/9	103/53	../..	../..	74	../..
52	Kenya	44/19	70/49	78/5	64/30	97/91	../..	62	25/16
53	Zimbabwe	63/47	81/67	43/14	../..	132/126	../..	79*	56/38
54	Honduras	55/50	61/58	366/64	68/67	103/102	../..	27*	../..
55	Algeria	39/11	63/37	221/72	55/37	104/83	95/78	83*	../..
56	Tunisia	44/17	68/41	219/56	88/43	127/108	100/89	78	46/33
57	Guatemala	51/37	63/47	44/26	50/39	../..	../..	38	../..
58	Saudi Arabia	15/2	35ˣ/12ˣ	321/269	22/2	77/61	63/46	79	51/33
59	South Africa	../..	../..	309/93	94/85	../..	../..	..	../..
60	Nicaragua	58/57	../..	244/58	65/66	../..	../..	27	../..
61	Turkey	69/35	86ˣ/62ˣ	130/148	90/58	119/112	../..	85*	53/31
62	Iraq	50/18	90/87	189/57	94/36	108/92	92/81	65*	69/39
63	Botswana	37/44	73/69	126/..	35/48	98/109	83/93	80*	27/31
64	Viet Nam	../..	88*/80*	100/33	../..	107/94	../..	50*	44/41

Note: nations are listed in descending order of their 1986 under-five mortality rates (see table 1)

		Adult literacy rate		No. of radio/television receivers per 1,000 population 1985	Primary-school enrolment ratio			% of grade 1 enrolment completing primary school 1980–86	Secondary-school enrolment ratio 1983–86 male/female
		1970 male/female	1985 male/female		1960 (gross) male/female	1983–86 (gross) male/female	1983–86 (net) male/female		
	Middle U5MR countries (26–94) Median	76/69	89/85	193/97	98/90	105/102	. ./. .	67	56/55
65	Madagascar	56/43	74/62	. ./5	58/45	125/118	. ./. .	30*	43/30
66	Ecuador	75/68	85/80	293/64	87/79	117/117	. ./. .	50*	51/53
67	Papua New Guinea	39/24	55/35	63/. .	59/7	68/55	. ./. .	67*	15/8
68	Brazil	69/63	79/76	391/184	97/93	108/99	. ./. .	20*	. ./. .
69	Burma	85/57	. ./. .	81/(.)	61/52	. ./. .	. ./. .	27*	. ./. .
70	El Salvador	61/53	75/69	342/63	82/77	. ./. .	. ./. .	68*	. ./. .
71	Dominican Rep.	69/65	78/77	160/80	99/98	. ./. .	. ./. .	88*	. ./. .
72	Philippines	83/80	86/85	65/28	98/93	105/106	94/95	64*	63/66
73	Mexico	78/69	92/88	190/108	82/77	116/114	. ./. .	66*	56/54
74	Colombia	79/76	89/87	139/96	77/77	116/119	. ./. .	37x	50/51
75	Syrian Arab Rep.	60/20	76/43	238/57	89/39	116/101	99/91	67*	72/49
76	Paraguay	84/75	91/85	163/23	105/90	104/98	87/85	48x	31/30
77	Mongolia	87/74	93x/86x	131/31	79/78	104/106	. ./. .	95y	84/92
78	Jordan	64/29	87/63	225/68	94/59	98/99	88/88	97	80/78
79	Lebanon	79/58	86/69	787/300	105/99	105/95	. ./. .	66*	57/56
80	Thailand	86/72	94/88	175/97	88/79	93*/93*	. ./. .	64*	35*/35*
81	Albania	. ./. .	. ./. .	162/76	102/86	99/95	. ./. .	. .	74/64
82	China	. ./. .	82/56	113/ 9	. ./. .	132/114	. ./. .	66*	45/32
83	Sri Lanka	85/69	91/83	. ./28	100/90	105/102	. ./. .	91	60/67
84	Venezuela	79/71	88/85	422/130	100/100	109/108	. ./. .	68y	41/50
85	United Arab Emirates	24/7	58x/38x	264/98	. ./. .	99/99	77/78	97	53/65
86	Guyana	94/89	97/95	. ./. .	107/106	. ./. .	. ./. .	84	. ./. .
87	Argentina	94/92	96/95	654/213	98/99	107/108	. ./. .	66y	66/75
88	Malaysia	71/48	81/66	424/101	108/83	100/99	. ./. .	97	52/53
89	Panama	81/81	89/88	183/160	98/94	107/102	88/89	73	56/63
90	Korea, Dem. Rep. of	. ./. .	. ./. .	172/10	. ./. .	. ./. .	. ./. .	. .	. ./. .
91	Korea, Rep. of	94/81	96x/88x	936/187	99/89	94/94	92/92	94	98/93
92	Uruguay	93/93	93x/94x	598/166	111/111	111/109	. ./. .	88	. ./. .
93	Mauritius	77/59	89/77	238/102	103/93	105/106	96/98	. .	53/49
94	Romania	96/91	. ./. .	141/173	101/95	98/97	. ./. .	. .	74/76
95	Yugoslavia	92/76	97/86	193/175	113/108	96/96	. ./. .	98	84/80
96	USSR	98/97	. ./. .	656/296	100/100	. ./. .	. ./. .	. .	. ./. .
	Low U5MR countries (25 and under) Median	94/89	97/93	470/290	105/103	102/101	96/96	95	81/85
97	Chile	90/88	97x/96x	332/145	111/107	108/106	. ./. .	33*	63/69
98	Trinidad and Tobago	95/89	97/95	321/270	89/87	93/96	89/92	78	74/79
99	Jamaica	96/97	90x/93x	385/92	92/93	106/107	93/96	80	56/60
100	Kuwait	65/42	76/63	274/235	131/102	102/99	86/83	98	85/80
101	Costa Rica	88/87	94/93	85/77	97/95	101/100	86/87	75	39/43
102	Portugal	78/65	89/80	212/157	132/129	120/119	98/96	88x	43/51
103	Bulgaria	94/89	. ./. .	222/187	94/92	102/101	98/97	87	90/91
104	Hungary	98/98	. ./. .	574/397	103/100	98/99	96/98	93	71/72
105	Poland	98/97	. ./. .	271/255	110/107	102/100	99/99	94	73/79
106	Cuba	86/87	96x/96x	327/197	109/109	108/101	94/94	86	82/88
107	Greece	93/76	97/88	405/174	104/101	106/106	91/92	93	87/84
108	Czechoslovakia	. ./. .	. ./. .	272/280	93/93	97/98	. ./. .	94	. ./. .
109	Israel	93/83	97/93	470/259	99/97	98/101	. ./. .	. .	73/80
110	New Zealand	. ./. .	. ./. .	904/290	110/106	107/106	100/100	. .	84/86
111	USA	99/99	. ./. .	2101/798	. ./. .	101/101	96/96	. .	99/98
112	Austria	. ./. .	. ./. .	620/435	106/104	100/98	. ./. .	95	77/81
113	Belgium	99/99	. ./. .	457/300	111/108	94/96	93/95	75	94/97
114	German Dem. Rep.	. ./. .	. ./. .	596/363	111/113	102/100	. ./. .	. .	80/77
115	Italy	95/93	98/96	259/253	112/109	99/99	. ./. .	100	74/73
116	Singapore	82/55	93/79	281/195	121/101	118/113	100/100	90	70/73
117	Germany, Fed. Rep. of	. ./. .	. ./. .	430/373	. ./. .	96/96	. ./. .	96	73/75
118	Ireland	. ./. .	. ./. .	568/252	107/112	100/100	. ./. .	. .	91/101
119	Spain	93/87	97/92	298/270	106/116	108/107	100/100	95	88/91
120	United Kingdom	. ./. .	. ./. .	1016/437	92/92	103/103	100/100	. .	83/87
121	Australia	. ./. .	. ./. .	1274/446	103/103	106/105	97/97	. .	94/97
122	Hong Kong	90/64	95/81	586/236	93/79	106/104	95/96	98	66/72
123	France	99/98	. ./. .	879/394	144/143	108/106	96/96	95	80/87
124	Canada	. ./. .	. ./. .	863/516	108/105	106/104	. ./. .	. .	102/103
125	Denmark	. ./. .	. ./. .	416/386	103/103	98/99	. ./. .	99	104/103
126	Japan	99/99	. ./. .	787/580	103/102	101/102	100/100	100	95/97
127	Netherlands	. ./. .	. ./. .	828/462	105/104	94/96	85/88	95	103/100
128	Switzerland	. ./. .	. ./. .	821/400	118/118	. ./. .	. ./. .	99	. ./. .
129	Norway	. ./. .	. ./. .	780/330	100/100	97/97	97/97	100	95/100
130	Finland	. ./. .	. ./. .	988/470	100/95	104/103	. ./. .	. .	95/110
131	Sweden	. ./. .	. ./. .	868/390	95/96	97/99	. ./. .	98	79/88

TABLE 5: DEMOGRAPHIC INDICATORS

		Population under 16/under 5 (millions) 1986	Population annual growth rate (%)		Crude death rate		Crude birth rate		Life expectancy		Total fertility rate 1986	% population urbanized 1985	Average annual growth rate of urban population (%)		Contraceptive prevalence (%) 1981-85
			1965-80	1980-85	1960	1986	1960	1986	1960	1986			1965-80	1980-85	
	Very high U5MR countries (over 170) **Median**	228T/88T	2.5	2.6	28	19	48	47	38	48	6.5	24	6.1	5.0	2
1	Afghanistan	7.6/2.9	2.4		30	25	52	51	34	39	6.7	19	6.0	. .	2ˣ
2	Mali	4.0/1.6	2.6	2.3	29	21	50	50	35	44	6.7	18	4.9	4.5	1
3	Sierra Leone	1.6/0.6	2.2	2.6	35	28	48	47	30	36	6.1	29	4.3	5.1	4
4	Malawi	3.5/1.4	2.9	3.1	28	20	53	53	38	47	7.0	13	7.8	. .	1
5	Ethiopia	21.1/8.4	2.7	2.5	28	23	51	50	36	42	6.7	12	6.6	3.7	2
6	Guinea	2.8/1.1	1.9	2.4	33	22	48	47	33	42	6.2	23	6.6	4.3	1
7	Somalia	2.2/0.9	3.3	2.9	28	23	47	48	36	42	6.6	35	6.1	5.4	. .
8	Mozambique	6.5/2.5	2.5	2.6	21	19	45	45	40	47	6.1	20	11.8	5.3	. .
9	Burkina Faso	3.3/1.3	2.0	2.6	31	19	50	48	35	47	6.5	8	3.4	5.3	1
10	Angola	4.2/1.6	2.8	2.5	31	21	50	47	33	44	6.4	25	6.4	5.8	1
11	Niger	3.1/1.2	2.7	3.0	31	21	46	51	35	44	7.1	17	6.9	7.0	1
12	Chad	2.3/0.9	2.0	2.3	30	20	46	44	35	45	5.9	28	9.2	3.9	1
13	Guinea-Bissau	0.4/0.1	. .	. .	28	20	41	41	36	45	5.4	28	. .	. .	. .
14	Central African Rep.	1.2/0.5	1.8	2.5	30	21	44	44	37	45	5.9	43	4.8	3.9	. .
15	Senegal	3.1/1.2	2.5	2.9	27	20	48	47	37	45	6.5	37	4.1	4.0	4ˣ
16	Mauritania	0.9/0.4	2.2	2.1	28	20	51	50	36	46	6.9	36	12.4	3.4	1
17	Liberia	1.1/0.4	3.0	3.4	24	16	46	48	40	51	6.9	40	6.2	4.3	1
18	Rwanda	3.2/1.3	3.3	3.2	22	18	51	51	42	48	7.4	7	6.3	6.7	10
19	Kampuchea	2.6/1.3	0.3		21	17	45	43	42	48	4.8	11	1.9	. .	. .
20	Yemen	3.5/1.3	2.8	2.5	29	17	50	48	37	50	6.9	21	10.7	7.3	1ˣ
21	Yemen, Dem.	1.0/0.4	2.0	2.6	29	16	50	47	37	50	6.6	41	3.2	4.9	. .
22	Bhutan	0.6/0.2	1.5	2.2	25	17	43	37	38	48	5.4	5	3.7	5.2	. .
23	Nepal	7.6/2.7	2.4	2.4	26	17	46	40	38	48	6.0	8	5.1	5.6	15
24	Burundi	2.3/0.9	1.9	2.7	25	18	44	46	42	48	6.4	6	1.8	2.7	1
25	Bangladesh	49.6/18.1	2.7	2.6	22	16	47	42	40	49	5.7	12	8.0	7.9	22
26	Benin	2.1/0.8	2.7	3.1	33	20	47	51	35	46	7.0	37	10.2	4.4	20
27	Sudan	10.5/4.0	3.0	2.7	25	16	47	45	39	50	6.4	21	5.1	4.8	5ˣ
28	Tanzania, U. Rep. of	11.9/4.7	3.3	3.5	24	14	51	50	41	53	7.1	24	8.7	8.3	1
29	Bolivia	3.0/1.1	2.5	2.8	22	15	46	43	43	53	6.1	49	2.9	5.6	26
30	Nigeria	49.9/19.7	2.5	3.3	24	16	52	51	40	50	7.1	24	4.8	5.2	5
31	Haiti	3.1/1.1	2.0	1.8	23	13	45	41	42	54	5.6	28	4.0	4.1	7
32	Gabon	0.4/0.2	. .	. .	25	17	31	37	40	51	4.9	42	. .	. .	. .
33	Uganda	8.1/3.2	2.9	3.0	21	16	50	50	43	51	6.9	10	4.1	3.0	1
	High U5MR countries (95-170) **Median**	624T/216T	2.9	3.2	21	12	48	42	45	57	5.9	43	5.3	4.8	24
34	Pakistan	47.0/17.6	3.1	3.1	24	14	49	41	43	52	5.5	30	4.3	4.8	8
35	Zaire	14.6/5.6	2.8	3.0	22	15	47	45	42	52	6.1	37	7.2	8.4	1
36	Lao People's Dem. Rep.	1.9/0.7	1.4	2.0	19	14	42	39	44	52	5.5	16	4.8	5.6	. .
37	Oman	0.6/0.2	3.6	4.8	28	13	51	45	40	55	6.9	9	8.1	7.3	. .
38	Iran (Islamic Rep. of)	20.5/7.4	3.2	2.9	19	11	53	39	50	59	5.3	53	5.5	4.6	23
39	Cameroon	4.6/1.8	2.7	3.2	24	15	44	43	40	53	5.8	44	8.1	7.0	3ˣ
40	Togo	1.4/0.6	3.0	3.3	27	15	48	45	39	52	6.1	23	7.2	6.4	. .
41	India	297.4/99.0	2.3	2.2	21	11	42	29	44	57	3.9	26	3.6	3.9	34
42	Côte d'Ivoire	4.9/1.9	5.0	3.8	26	15	44	45	39	52	6.6	43	8.7	6.9	3
43	Ghana	6.9/2.7	2.2	3.3	21	14	47	47	45	54	6.5	32	3.4	3.9	10
44	Lesotho	0.7/0.3	2.3	2.7	24	15	41	41	40	51	5.8	17	14.6	5.3	5
45	Zambia	3.4/1.3	3.1	3.5	23	14	50	48	42	53	6.8	51	7.1	5.5	1
46	Egypt	20.0/7.2	2.6	2.8	21	10	45	34	46	60	4.5	47	2.9	3.4	30
47	Peru	8.6/3.0	2.7	2.3	19	10	47	35	48	61	4.6	68	4.1	3.8	43
48	Libyan Arab Jamahiriya	1.8/0.7	4.5	3.9	19	10	49	44	47	60	7.0	66	9.7	6.7	. .
49	Morocco	9.6/3.3	2.5	2.5	21	10	50	33	47	60	4.6	46	4.2	4.2	27
50	Indonesia	68.5/22.6	2.3	2.1	23	12	44	29	41	56	3.7	26	4.7	2.3	38
51	Congo	0.8/0.3	2.7	3.1	25	18	45	44	38	48	6.0	40	3.5	3.6	. .
52	Kenya	11.8/4.7	3.9	4.1	24	13	57	54	42	55	8.0	20	9.0	6.3	17
53	Zimbabwe	4.5/1.8	3.1	3.7	19	11	47	47	45	57	6.6	25	7.5	5.0	40
54	Honduras	2.2/0.8	3.2	3.5	19	9	51	40	47	62	5.9	41	5.5	5.2	35
55	Algeria	10.7/3.9	3.0	3.3	21	9	51	42	47	62	6.5	43	3.8	3.7	7
56	Tunisia	3.0/1.0	2.1	2.3	19	9	47	31	48	62	4.3	58	4.2	3.7	42
57	Guatemala	3.9/1.5	2.8	2.9	20	9	49	41	46	61	5.9	40	3.6	4.2	25
58	Saudi Arabia	5.6/2.1	4.6	4.2	23	8	49	41	44	63	6.9	73	8.5	6.1	. .
59	South Africa	14.4/5.4	2.3	2.5	21	13	41	38	44	55	5.0	56	2.6	3.3	48
60	Nicaragua	1.7/0.6	3.1	3.4	18	8	51	42	47	63	5.6	57	4.6	4.5	9
61	Turkey	19.2/6.5	2.4	2.5	16	9	43	30	51	64	3.7	46	4.3	4.4	38ˣ
62	Iraq	8.1/3.0	3.4	3.6	20	8	49	42	49	64	6.2	71	5.3	6.3	14ˣ
63	Botswana	0.6/0.2	4.2	3.5	20	12	52	49	46	56	6.5	20	15.4	4.5	29
64	Viet Nam	25.2/8.2	. .	2.6	23	9	41	30	44	61	3.9	21	4.1	3.4	. .

Note: nations are listed in descending order of their 1986 under-five mortality rates (see table 1)

		Population under 16/under 5 (millions) 1986	Population annual growth rate (%)		Crude death rate		Crude birth rate		Life expectancy		Total fertility rate 1986	% population urbanized 1985	Average annual growth rate of urban population (%)		Contraceptive prevalence (%) 1981-85
			1965-80	1980-85	1960	1986	1960	1986	1960	1986			1965-80	1980-85	
	Middle U5MR countries (26–94) **Median**	662T/205T	2.5	2.3	14	7	43	29	55	68	3.6	53	4.5	3.4	51
65	Madagascar	4.8/1.8	2.5	3.2	23	15	44	44	41	51	6.1	22	5.7	5.3	. .
66	Ecuador	4.2/1.5	3.1	2.9	15	8	46	36	53	65	4.8	53	5.1	3.7	40
67	Papua New Guinea	1.6/0.6	2.4	2.6	23	12	44	36	41	54	5.4	15	8.4	4.9	4
68	Brazil	53.0/18.2	2.5	2.3	13	8	43	29	55	65	3.6	74	4.5	4.0	65
69	Burma	14.9/4.9	2.2	2.0	21	10	42	29	44	60	3.8	24	2.8	2.8	5
70	El Salvador	2.7/1.0	2.7	1.0	17	7	48	38	50	67	5.2	39	3.5	4.0	47
71	Dominican Rep.	2.7/0.9	2.7	2.4	17	7	49	31	51	64	3.8	57	5.3	4.2	47
72	Philippines	23.6/8.0	2.8	2.5	15	8	46	31	46	63	4.1	40	4.0	3.2	33
73	Mexico	35.6/11.9	3.2	2.6	12	7	45	32	57	67	4.2	70	4.5	3.6	48
74	Colombia	11.5/4.0	2.2	1.9	13	7	45	30	55	65	3.7	68	3.5	2.8	51ˣ
75	Syrian Arab Rep.	5.5/2.1	3.4	3.6	18	7	47	46	50	65	6.9	50	4.5	5.5	20ˣ
76	Paraguay	1.7/0.6	2.9	3.3	13	7	43	35	56	66	4.6	45	3.2	3.7	39ˣ
77	Mongolia	0.9/0.3	3.0	2.6	15	8	41	35	52	64	4.9	51	4.5	3.3	. .
78	Jordan	1.9/0.7	2.6	3.7	20	7	47	46	47	66	7.3	65	5.3	4.0	26
79	Lebanon	1.1/0.4	1.6	. .	14	8	43	29	60	67	3.5	81	4.6	. .	53ˣ
80	Thailand	19.8/6.3	2.7	2.1	15	8	39	24	52	64	3.0	20	4.6	3.2	63
81	Albania	1.2/0.4	2.5	2.1	11	6	41	27	62	72	3.4	. .	3.4	3.3	. .
82	China	334.6/94.0	2.2	1.2	19	7	37	19	47	69	2.2	21	2.6	3.3	71
83	Sri Lanka	6.0/2.1	1.8	1.4	9	6	36	25	62	70	3.0	21	2.3	8.4	57
84	Venezuela	7.4/2.6	3.5	2.9	10	5	45	31	60	70	3.9	87	4.5	3.5	49ˣ
85	United Arab Emirates	0.5/0.2	15.9	6.2	19	4	46	26	53	69	5.6	77	18.9	5.5	. .
86	Guyana	0.4/0.1	. .	. .	10	5	42	26	60	70	2.9	33	. .	. .	35ˣ
87	Argentina	10.1/3.5	1.6	1.6	9	9	24	24	65	70	3.3	85	2.2	1.9	74
88	Malaysia	6.3/2.2	2.5	2.5	24	6	44	28	54	68	3.5	39	4.5	4.0	51
89	Panama	0.9/0.3	2.6	2.2	10	5	41	27	61	72	3.2	53	3.4	2.6	59
90	Korea, Dem. Rep. of	8.5/2.9	2.7	2.5	13	6	41	29	54	69	3.7	65	4.6	3.8	. .
91	Korea, Rep. of	13.9/4.5	1.9	1.5	14	6	43	23	54	69	2.5	66	5.7	2.5	70
92	Uruguay	0.9/0.3	0.4	0.7	10	10	22	19	68	71	2.7	85	0.7	0.9	. .
93	Mauritius	0.4/0.1	1.7	1.3	10	6	44	23	59	68	2.5	42	4.0	2.1	75
94	Romania	6.2/1.9	1.1	0.5	9	10	20	17	65	71	2.4	49	3.4	1.0	58ˣ
95	Yugoslavia	5.9/1.8	0.9	0.7	10	9	23	15	63	72	2.0	47	3.0	2.5	55ˣ
96	USSR	74.1/25.1	0.9	0.9	7	9	24	19	68	72	2.4	66	2.2	1.6	. .
	Low U5MR countries (25 and under) **Median**	204T/63T	0.9	0.7	9	10	21	15	69	74	1.9	76	2.0	1.4	71
97	Chile	3.9/1.3	1.8	1.7	12	7	37	22	57	71	2.5	84	2.6	2.1	43
98	Trinidad and Tobago	0.4/0.1	1.3	1.6	8	7	38	24	64	70	2.7	65	5.0	3.3	55ˣ
99	Jamaica	0.9/0.3	1.1	1.6	10	6	39	27	63	74	3.0	55	3.4	3.2	52
100	Kuwait	0.8/0.3	7.0	4.5	10	3	44	35	60	73	5.9	94	8.2	5.1	. .
101	Costa Rica	1.0/0.4	2.8	2.7	10	4	47	29	62	74	3.3	51	3.7	3.8	68
102	Portugal	2.7/0.8	0.6	0.7	7	9	24	17	63	73	2.1	32	2.0	3.3	70ˣ
103	Bulgaria	2.2/0.7	0.5	0.2	9	11	18	15	69	72	2.2	67	2.8	1.7	76ˣ
104	Hungary	2.4/0.7	0.4	-0.1	10	13	16	12	68	71	1.8	57	1.8	1.3	74ˣ
105	Poland	10.0/3.2	0.8	0.9	8	10	24	17	67	72	2.2	61	1.8	1.6	75ˣ
106	Cuba	2.8/0.8	1.5	0.8	9	7	32	18	64	74	2.0	72	2.7	0.8	60
107	Greece	2.3/0.7	0.7	0.6	8	10	19	15	69	75	2.1	61	2.5	1.9	. .
108	Czechoslovakia	4.0/1.2	0.5	0.3	10	12	17	15	70	72	2.1	66	1.9	1.4	. .
109	Israel	1.4/0.5	2.8	1.8	6	7	27	22	69	75	2.9	91	3.5	2.4	. .
110	New Zealand	0.9/0.3	1.3	0.9	9	8	26	16	71	74	1.9	84	1.5	0.9	. .
111	USA	56.1/18.8	1.0	1.0	9	9	24	16	70	75	1.9	74	1.2	2.3	68
112	Austria	1.5/0.5	0.3	0.0	12	12	18	12	69	74	1.6	56	0.1	0.7	71
113	Belgium	2.0/0.6	0.3	0.1	12	12	17	12	70	74	1.6	96	0.5	0.4	81
114	German Dem. Rep.	3.5/1.2	-0.2	-0.1	13	13	17	14	70	73	1.9	77	0.1	0.6	. .
115	Italy	11.8/3.2	0.6	0.3	10	11	18	11	69	75	1.6	68	1.0	0.9	78ˣ
116	Singapore	0.7/0.2	1.6	1.2	8	6	38	17	65	73	1.7	100	1.6	1.2	74
117	Germany, Fed. Rep. of	10.1/3.1	0.3	-0.2	11	12	17	11	70	74	1.4	86	0.8	0.1	. .
118	Ireland	1.1/0.4	1.4	0.9	12	9	21	22	70	74	3.0	57	2.2	2.7	60ˣ
119	Spain	9.9/2.8	1.0	0.7	9	9	21	15	69	75	2.1	76	2.4	1.6	51ˣ
120	United Kingdom	11.7/3.7	0.2	0.1	12	12	17	13	71	74	1.8	92	0.5	0.3	83
121	Australia	4.0/1.2	1.8	1.4	9	8	22	16	71	76	1.9	86	0.2	1.4	67ˣ
122	Hong Kong	1.4/0.5	2.2	1.4	7	6	35	15	65	76	1.9	93	2.3	1.3	72ˣ
123	France	12.4/3.8	0.7	0.6	12	11	18	14	70	75	1.9	73	2.7	1.0	79ˣ
124	Canada	5.9/1.9	1.3	1.1	8	8	27	15	71	76	1.7	76	1.5	1.7	73
125	Denmark	1.0/0.3	0.5	0.1	9	12	17	11	72	75	1.5	86	1.1	0.3	63ˣ
126	Japan	27.7/7.7	1.2	0.7	7	7	18	12	68	77	1.8	77	2.1	1.8	57
127	Netherlands	3.0/0.9	0.9	0.4	8	9	21	12	73	76	1.5	88	1.5	0.9	78
128	Switzerland	1.2/0.4	0.5	0.3	10	10	18	11	71	77	1.5	58	1.2	0.9	70ˣ
129	Norway	0.9/0.3	0.6	0.3	9	11	18	12	73	76	1.6	73	5.0	0.9	71ˣ
130	Finland	1.0/0.3	0.3	0.5	9	10	19	13	68	75	1.6	65	2.5	2.9	80ˣ
131	Sweden	1.6/0.5	0.5	0.1	10	12	14	10	73	77	1.5	84	1.0	1.2	78

TABLE 6: ECONOMIC INDICATORS

		GNP per capita (US $) 1985	GNP per capita average annual growth rate (%)		Rate of inflation (%) 1980-85	% of population below absolute poverty level 1977-85 urban/rural	% of central gov't expenditure allocated to health/education/defence 1985	ODA inflow in millions US $ (1984)/ as a % of recipient GNP (1985)	Debt service as a % of exports of goods and services	
			1965-80	1980-85		urban/rural			1970	1985
	Very high U5MR countries (over 170) Median	280	0.2	−1.0	9.7	35/65	5.5/14.0 /13.8	184/10.6	4.2	16.6
1	Afghanistan	. .	1.4	−3.0	7.4	18/36	4.0ʸ/17.0ʸ/18.0ʸ	17/. .	1.4	16.6
2	Mali	150	1.1	−0.2	25.0	27ˣ/48ˣ	7.5/16.5 /4.4	380/34.9	10.4	5.7
3	Sierra Leone	350	1.5	−0.6	11.4	. ./65	7.9/12.3 /5.7	66/5.5	7.7	. .
4	Malawi	170	0.2	−2.0	2.6	25/85	. ./. . /. .	113/11.0	11.4	10.9
5	Ethiopia	110				60ˣ/65ˣ		710/15.1		
6	Guinea	320	0.8	−1.4	8.3	. ./. .	. ./. . /. .	119/6.5		
7	Somalia	280	−0.7	0.6	45.4	40/70	. ./. . /. .	354/14.5	2.1	44.8
8	Mozambique	160		−13.6	25.8	. ./. .	7.0ˣ/16.0ˣ/. .	300/9.2		
9	Burkina Faso	150	1.3	−1.3	7.2	. ./. .	5.5/16.9 /18.2	197/18.4	6.8	. .
10	Angola	470ˣ		0.1		. ./. .	. ./. . /. .	92/. .		
11	Niger	250	−2.1	−6.7	8.5	. ./35ˣ	. ./. . /. .	305/19.8	4.0	26.7
12	Chad	80ˣ	−2.3	1.8		30ˣ/56ˣ	. ./. . /. .	182/. .	4.2	. .
13	Guinea−Bissau	180	−1.5	1.9	30.4		. ./14.0ˣ/. .	. ./. .		
14	Central African Rep.	260	−0.2	−1.5	10.8	. ./91		105/15.9	5.1	11.8
15	Senegal	370	−0.6	0.0	9.7	. ./. .		295/12.2	2.9	9.0
16	Mauritania	420	0.1	−0.7	8.1	. ./. .	. ./. . /. .	205/31.2	3.3	19.0
17	Liberia	470	−1.4	−6.4	1.6	. ./23	5.5/16.5 /9.5	91/8.8	. .	3.8
18	Rwanda	280	1.8	−1.5	7.6	30/90ˣ	. ./. . /. .	181/10.7	1.2	4.3
19	Kampuchea	. .	. .	. .		. ./. .	. ./. . /. .	13/. .		
20	Yemen	550	5.3	0.9	9.7	. ./. .	4.4/20.6 /30.1	288/7.0	. .	55.8
21	Yemen, Dem.	530	. .		5.7	. ./20	. ./. . /. .	112/10.4	0.0	42.3
22	Bhutan	160		3.4ˣ				24/12.9		
23	Nepal	160	0.1	0.8	8.4	55/61	5.0/12.1 /6.2	236/10.1	. .	4.0
24	Burundi	230	1.9	−0.8	6.6	55/85	. ./. . /. .	143/13.7	2.3	16.6
25	Bangladesh	150	0.4	0.9	11.5	86/86	2.0ʸ/ 4.0ʸ/. .	1142/7.1	. .	16.7
26	Benin	260	0.2	0.1	9.7	. ./65	6.1/. . /33.6	96/9.5	2.3	
27	Sudan	300	(.)	−4.2	31.7	. ./85ˣ	. ./. . /. .	1129/15.6	10.7	15.6
28	Tanzania, U. Rep. of	290	(.)	−3.1	19.6	15ˣ/25ˣ	4.9/ 7.2 /13.8	487/7.9	5.2	16.7
29	Bolivia	470	−0.2	−7.0	569.1	. ./85ˣ	1.5/12.2 /5.4	202/6.2	11.3	29.1
30	Nigeria	800	2.2	−7.3	11.4	. ./. .	3.0/ 5.0 /12.0	32/(.)	4.2	30.8
31	Haiti	310	0.7	−2.5	7.0	55/78	5.7/ 6.0 /8.4	153/8.0	7.7	5.8
32	Gabon	3670	1.5	−1.2	10.1	. ./. .	. ./. . /. .	. ./. .		
33	Uganda	230	−2.6	2.2		. ./. .	2.5/11.7 /16.7	184/. .	2.9	
	High U5MR countries (95–170) Median	770	2.2	0.1	10.4	30/45	4.5/14.0 /12.4	161/3.5	7.2	19.9
34	Pakistan	380	2.6	2.8	8.1	32/29	1.1/ 2.9 /32.3	750/2.2	23.4	29.5
35	Zaire	170	−2.1	−3.8	55.3	. ./80ˣ	1.8/ 0.8 /5.2	324/7.5	4.4	8.6
36	Lao People's Dem. Rep.	. .	. .	. .	57.0	. ./. .	. ./ 9.0ʸ/. .	37/2.7		
37	Oman	6730	5.7	0.5	4.9	. ./. .	4.2/ 7.7 /43.0	78/1.0	. .	4.8
38	Iran (Islamic Rep. of)	. .	. .	7.1ˣ		. ./. .	7.4/16.2 /10.2	17/. .	. .	. .
39	Cameroon	810	3.6	4.5	11.8	15/40	5.1/14.4 /8.8	160/2.1	3.2	10.0
40	Togo	230	0.3	−5.6	6.9	42/. .	3.6/11.7 /6.9	114/17.5	3.0	27.5
41	India	270	1.7	3.1	7.8	40/51	2.4/ 1.9 /18.8	1470/0.7	23.7	9.3
42	Côte d'Ivoire	660	0.9	−5.2	10.0	30ˣ/26ˣ	. ./. . /. .	125/1.9	7.0	17.4
43	Ghana	380	−2.2	−3.9	57.0	59ˣ/37ˣ	9.8/18.0 /7.5	204/4.1	5.2	12.2
44	Lesotho	470	6.5	3.4	11.4	50/55	5.8/14.8 /11.8	94/16.5	. .	6.2
45	Zambia	390	−1.6	−4.1	14.7	25/. .	. ./. . /. .	329/15.4	6.3	10.2
46	Egypt	610	3.1	1.3	11.0	21ˣ/25ˣ	2.4/10.6 /17.5	1759/6.1	36.8	30.9
47	Peru	1010	0.2	−4.2	98.6	49/. .	. ./. . /. .	316/2.0	11.6	7.9
48	Libyan Arab Jamahiriya	7170	−1.3	−9.1	−0.3	. ./. .	. ./. . /. .	5/(.)	. .	. .
49	Morocco	560	2.2	0.1	7.8	28/45	3.1/19.2 /14.9	834/7.5	8.6	32.7
50	Indonesia	530	4.8	2.3	10.7	26/44	2.5/11.3 /12.9	603/0.7	. .	19.9
51	Congo	1110	3.8	4.9	12.6	. ./. .	. ./. . /. .	71/3.5	. .	19.6
52	Kenya	290	1.9	−1.7	10.0	10/55	6.7/19.8 /12.9	439/7.9	5.8	25.5
53	Zimbabwe	680	1.6	0.0	13.2	. ./. .	6.2/20.4 /16.2	237/4.9	. .	32.2
54	Honduras	720	0.4	−2.6	5.4	14/55	. ./. . /. .	276/8.7	3.1	17.6
55	Algeria	2550	3.6	1.7	6.9	20/. .	. ./. . /. .	173/0.3	3.9	33.3
56	Tunisia	1190	4.0	1.4	10.0	20/15	6.5/14.3 /7.9	162/2.1	19.5	24.9
57	Guatemala	1250	1.7	−4.3	7.4	66/74	. ./. . /. .	83/0.8	7.4	21.3
58	Saudi Arabia	8850	5.3	−7.3	−3.2	. ./. .	6.0ʸ/14.0ʸ/36.0ʸ	29/(.)	. .	. .
59	South Africa	2010	1.1	−1.6	13.0	. ./. .	. ./. . /. .	. ./. .	10.5	. .
60	Nicaragua	770	−2.1	−3.1	33.8	21/19	. ./. . /. .	102/4.0		
61	Turkey	1080	2.6	2.1	37.1	. ./. .	1.8/10.0 /10.9	176/0.3	22.1	30.8
62	Iraq	3020ˣ	. .	. .		. ./40ˣ	4.0ˣ/ 3.0ˣ/. .	26/. .		
63	Botswana	840	8.3	7.4	5.2	40/55	4.8/17.5 /6.8	97/13.7	. .	5.4
64	Viet Nam	. .	. .	. .		. ./. .	6.2ˣ/ 7.0ˣ/. .	114/. .		

Note: nations are listed in descending order of their 1986 under-five mortality rates (see table 1)

74

		GNP per capita (US $) 1985	GNP per capita average annual growth rate (%)		Rate of inflation (%) 1980–85	% of population below absolute poverty level 1977–85 urban/rural	% of central gov't. expenditure allocated to health/education/defence 1985	ODA inflow in millions US $ (1985)/ as a % of recipient GNP (1985)	Debt service as a % of exports of goods and services	
			1965–80	1980–85					1970	1985
	Middle U5MR countries (26–94) Median	1440	2.9	−0.8	10.5	21/39	5.9/12.1 /11.3	141/1.5	9.3	16.0
65	Madagascar	240	−1.9	−6.1	19.4	50/50	../.. /..	182/8.2	3.7	19.6
66	Ecuador	1160	3.5	−2.4	29.7	40/65	8.3/27.7 /11.3	136/1.2	8.6	28.8
67	Papua New Guinea	680	0.4	−1.6	5.5	10/75	9.0/19.1 /4.7	259/12.0	..	10.4
68	Brazil	1640	4.3	−1.5	147.7	../..	7.6/ 3.2 /4.0	123/0.1	12.5	26.5
69	Burma	190	2.4	3.3	2.6	40/40	7.3/11.7 /18.5	356/5.1	17.2	51.4
70	El Salvador	820	−0.2	−3.1	11.6	20/32	5.9/14.5 /20.3	345/9.4	3.6	16.3
71	Dominican Rep.	790	2.9	−0.8	14.6	45/43	10.3/15.1 /8.4	222/5.2	4.4	16.1
72	Philippines	580	2.3	−3.4	19.3	32/41	6.0/20.1 /11.9	486/1.5	7.3	15.9
73	Mexico	2080	2.7	−2.1	62.2	../..	1.5/12.4 /2.7	145/0.1	23.6	37.0
74	Colombia	1320	2.9	−0.5	22.5	34/..	../.. /..	62/0.2	12.0	29.2
75	Syrian Arab Rep.	1570	4.0	−2.1	6.1	../..	../.. /..	639/3.9	11.2	14.8
76	Paraguay	860	3.9	−1.9	15.8	19/50	5.8/10.7 /10.2	50/1.8	11.8	12.9
77	Mongolia	..	..	..	..	../..	../.. /..	../..	..	..
78	Jordan	1560	5.8	1.5	3.9	14/17	4.2/11.3 /27.7	550/14.5	3.6	22.1
79	Lebanon	..	..	..	..	../..	../.. /..	94/..	..	..
80	Thailand	800	4.0	2.6	3.2	15/34	5.7/19.5 /20.2	481/1.3	3.4	14.7
81	Albania	..	..	..	..	../..	../.. /..	../..	..	..
82	China	310	4.8	8.6	2.4	../..	../.. /..	940/0.4	..	..
83	Sri Lanka	380	2.9	3.2	14.7	../..	3.6/ 6.4 /2.6	486/8.2	10.8	13.9
84	Venezuela	3080	0.5	−5.4	9.2	../..	7.6/17.7 /6.1	11/(.)	2.9	12.8
85	United Arab Emirates	19270	..	−7.7	−1.4	../..	6.2/ 9.7 /45.3	3/(.)	..	..
86	Guyana	500	−0.2	−7.3	9.4	../..	2.0*/ 3.0*/..	../..	..	..
87	Argentina	2130	0.2	−3.9	342.8	../..	1.8/ 9.5 /8.8	39/0.1	21.6	41.8
88	Malaysia	2000	4.4	1.8	3.1	13/38	../.. /..	229/0.8	3.7	22.3
89	Panama	2100	2.5	−0.2	3.7	21/30	../.. /..	69/1.5	7.7	6.9
90	Korea, Dem. Rep. of	..	..	..	..	../..	../.. /..	../..	..	..
91	Korea, Rep. of	2150	6.6	6.3	6.0	18/11	1.4/18.4 /29.7	−9/(.)	19.5	15.2
92	Uruguay	1650	1.4	−6.0	44.6	22*/..	4.1/ 6.4 /10.8	5/0.1	21.7	30.6
93	Mauritius	1090	2.7	2.3	8.5	12/12	7.6/13.8 /0.8	29/2.8	3.2	11.5
94	Romania	2560x	..	3.0x	..	../..	../.. /..	../..	..	13.6
95	Yugoslavia	2070	4.1	−0.5	45.1	../..	(.)/(.) /54.8	11/(.)	10.0	8.2
96	USSR	4550x	..	..	..	../..	../.. /..	../..	..	..
	Low U5MR countries (25 and under) Median	7300	2.5	0.9	8.6	../..	10.0/9.3 /6.7	40/0.2	3.7	24.9
97	Chile	1430	−0.2	−3.9	19.3	27*/55*	6.1/13.2 /11.5	40/0.3	19.1	26.2
98	Trinidad and Tobago	6020	2.3	−6.0	7.6	../39	../.. /..	7/0.1	4.5	7.1
99	Jamaica	940	−0.7	−3.1	18.3	../80	7.0y/15.0y/3.0y	169/10.0	2.8	36.5
100	Kuwait	14480	−0.3	−6.8	−3.6	../..	6.5/11.6 /14.6	4/(.)	..	..
101	Costa Rica	1300	1.4	−2.7	36.4	../..	22.5/19.4 /3.0	280/8.0	10.0	36.6
102	Portugal	1970	3.3	−0.5	22.7	../..	../.. /..	103/0.5	..	31.5
103	Bulgaria	4150x	..	..	..	../..	../.. /..	../..	..	..
104	Hungary	1950	5.8	1.7	5.6	../..	3.6/ 1.6 /6.9	../..	..	25.0
105	Poland	2050	..	..	35.2	../..	../.. /..	../..	..	..
106	Cuba	..	..	..	..	../..	../.. /..	18/..	..	..
107	Greece	3550	3.6	−0.3	20.6	../..	../.. /..	13/(.)	9.4	24.7
108	Czechoslovakia	5820x	..	..	..	../..	../.. /..	../..	..	..
109	Israel	4990	2.5	−0.7	196.3	../..	3.5/ 7.1 /27.8	1978/10.3	2.8	19.7
110	New Zealand	7010	1.4	1.8	9.8	../..	12.5/10.9 /4.7	../..	..	..
111	USA	16690	1.7	1.4	5.3	../..	11.3/ 1.8 /24.9	../..	(..	..
112	Austria	9120	3.5	1.7	4.9	../..	11.7/ 9.6 /3.0	../..	..	..
113	Belgium	8280	2.8	0.6	5.9	../..	1.7/12.9 /5.1	../..	..	..
114	German Dem. Rep.	7180x	..	..	..	../..	../.. /..	../..	..	..
115	Italy	6520	2.6	0.4	14.2	../..	12.1/ 7.7 /3.5	../..	..	..
116	Singapore	7420	7.6	6.4	3.1	../..	6.2/20.2 /20.1	24/0.1	0.6	2.4
117	Germany, Fed. Rep. of	10940	2.7	1.2	3.2	../..	18.7/ 0.7 /9.2	../..	..	..
118	Ireland	4850	2.2	−0.3	10.8	../..	13.2/11.7 /3.1	../..	..	..
119	Spain	4290	2.6	0.9	12.6	../..	0.6/ 6.0 /4.4	../..	..	..
120	United Kingdom	8460	1.6	2.1	6.4	../..	../.. /..	../..	..	..
121	Australia	10830	2.0	0.9	9.1	../..	9.5/ 7.5 /9.3	../..	..	..
122	Hong Kong	6230	6.1	4.4	7.9	../..	../.. /..	21/0.1	(.)	0.2
123	France	9540	2.8	0.3	9.5	../..	../.. /..	../..	..	..
124	Canada	13680	2.4	0.8	6.3	../..	6.4/ 3.5 /7.9	../..	..	..
125	Denmark	11200	1.8	2.0	8.1	../..	../.. /..	../..	..	..
126	Japan	11300	4.7	3.5	1.2	../..	../.. /..	../..	..	..
127	Netherlands	9290	2.0	0.3	3.5	../..	11.0/10.9 /5.3	../..	..	..
128	Switzerland	16370	1.4	1.3	4.5	../..	13.1/ 3.1 /10.3	../..	..	..
129	Norway	14370	3.3	3.2	8.5	../..	10.8/ 8.9 /8.2	../..	..	..
130	Finland	10890	3.3	2.1	8.6	../..	10.4/13.8 /5.1	../..	..	..
131	Sweden	11890	1.8	1.5	8.6	../..	1.2/ 8.6 /6.4	../..	..	..

TABLE 7: WOMEN

		Life expectancy females as % of males 1986	Adult literacy rate as % of males 1985	Enrolment ratios females as % of males 1983–86		% Contraceptive prevalence 1981–85	% Pregnant women immunized against tetanus 1985–86	% of births attended by trained health personnel 1984	Maternal mortality rate 1980–84
				Primary-school	Secondary-school				
	Very high U5MR countries (over 170) **Median**	**107.0**	**48.9**	**64.4**	**42.9**	**2**	**12**	**22**	**450**
1	Afghanistan	102.1	20.5	50.0	45.5	2x	10	. .	640x
2	Mali	107.5	47.8	58.6	40.0	1	3*	. .	. .
3	Sierra Leone	108.7	55.3	70.6x	47.8x	4	17x	25	450
4	Malawi	102.8	59.6	87.2	33.3	1	47*	59	250x
5	Ethiopia	107.9	. .	63.6	64.3	2	6*	58	. .
6	Guinea	107.9	42.5	45.5	33.3	1	17*	. .	. .
7	Somalia	107.9	33.3	56.3	52.2	. .	7	2	1100
8	Mozambique	104.1	40.0	84.9	44.4	1	59*	28	300x
9	Burkina Faso	107.2	28.6	57.1	42.9	1	1*	. .	1500x
10	Angola	107.5	. .	85.9x	. .	1	54*	15	. .
11	Niger	107.5	47.4	54.1	33.3	1	16*	47	420
12	Chad	107.4	27.5	38.2	18.2	1	3	. .	. .
13	Guinea-Bissau	107.4	37.0	49.3	22.2	. .	16*	. .	400
14	Central African Rep.	107.4	54.7	53.2x	33.3x	. .	20*	. .	600
15	Senegal	107.3	51.4	69.2	50.0	4x	8	. .	530x
16	Mauritania	107.2	. .	64.4x	31.6x	1	. .	23	. .
17	Liberia	106.9	48.9	61.0*	39.4x	1	16*	89	. .
18	Rwanda	107.0	54.1	96.8	66.7	10	26*	. .	210
19	Kampuchea	106.2	76.5*	80.0*	44.4*	. .	3*	. .	. .
20	Yemen	106.1	11.1	19.6	17.6	1x	3	12	. .
21	Yemen, Dem.	106.1	42.4	36.5	42.3	. .	5	10	100
22	Bhutan	96.9	. .	56.3	16.7	. .	4	3	. .
23	Nepal	96.9	30.8	56.9*	37.3*	15	13	10	850x
24	Burundi	107.0	60.5x	74.5	60.0	1	17	12	. .
25	Bangladesh	98.0	51.2	71.4	38.5	22	5	. .	600
26	Benin	107.2	43.2	50.0	41.4	20	82x	34	1680x
27	Sudan	105.1	42.4y	86.0*	68.4*	5x	6	20	. .
28	Tanzania, U. Rep. of	106.6	94.6y	103.0*	60.0*	1	58*	74	370x
29	Bolivia	108.8	77.4	89.5	85.0	26	1	. .	480x
30	Nigeria	107.0	57.4	78.6	. .	5	11	. .	1500
31	Haiti	106.2	87.5	93.3	89.5	7	56*	20	156
32	Gabon	106.9	75.7	97.6	66.7	. .	32	. .	124
33	Uganda	106.9	64.3	88.4x	45.5x	1	5*	. .	300
	High U5MR countries (95–170) **Median**	**105.9**	**70.0**	**87.8**	**64.4**	**24**	**22**	**60**	**145**
34	Pakistan	96.8	47.5	50.0*	38.1*	8	28	24	600
35	Zaire	107.0	57.0	75.6	40.7	1	35*	. .	800
36	Lao People's Dem. Rep.	105.5	82.6	78.2	65.2	. .	8*	. .	. .
37	Oman	104.8	25.5y	92.5	48.8	. .	70*	60	. .
38	Iran (Islamic Rep. of)	100.9	62.9	87.8	68.5	23	28	. .	. .
39	Cameroon	106.8	80.9	83.6	62.1	3x	17*	. .	141x
40	Togo	106.9	52.8	61.9	30.3	. .	64*	. .	84x
41	India	100.2	50.9	71.0	53.3	34	40	33	500
42	Côte d'Ivoire	106.9	58.5	70.7	44.4	3	32y	. .	. .
43	Ghana	106.9	67.2	78.7	60.0	10	8*	73	1074x
44	Lesotho	108.3	135.5	124.5	144.4	5	0*	28	. .
45	Zambia	106.8	79.8	95.5	56.5	1	38*	. .	109
46	Egypt	97.7	50.8	80.9	71.2	30	8*	24	80
47	Peru	106.6	85.7	96.0	89.7	43	6*	44	314
48	Libyan Arab Jamahiriya	105.8	61.7	. .	. .	. .	12	76	80x
49	Morocco	105.8	48.9	65.8	65.8	27	. .	. .	327
50	Indonesia	105.1	78.3	96.0	75.6	38	26	43*	800
51	Congo	107.0	77.5	. .	. .	. .	11*	. .	. .
52	Kenya	106.7	70.0	93.8	64.0	17	40	. .	168x
53	Zimbabwe	106.6	82.7	95.5	67.9	40	40*	69	145x
54	Honduras	105.9	95.1	99.0	. .	35	18	50	82x
55	Algeria	105.1	58.7	82.1	. .	7	. .	. .	129
56	Tunisia	101.6	60.3	89.0	71.7	42	11	60	. .
57	Guatemala	107.9	74.6	. .	. .	25	2*	. .	105
58	Saudi Arabia	106.0	34.3x	73.0	64.7	. .	. .	78	. .
59	South Africa	106.3	. .	. .	. .	48	. .	. .	. .
60	Nicaragua	104.2	. .	. .	. .	9	25*	. .	65x
61	Turkey	105.3	72.1x	94.1	58.5	38x	4*	78y	207x
62	Iraq	102.9	96.7	88.0	56.5	14x	43*	60	. .
63	Botswana	105.8	94.5	112.0	114.8	29	16	52y	300
64	Viet Nam	107.5	90.9	87.9	93.2	. .	. .	99	110

Note: nations are listed in descending order of their 1986 under-five mortality rates (see table 1)

		Life expectancy females as % of males 1986	Adult literacy rate as % of males 1985	Enrolment ratios females as % of males 1983–86		% Contraceptive prevalence 1981–85	% Pregnant women immunized against tetanus 1985–86	% of births attended by trained health personnel 1984	Maternal mortality rate 1980–84
				Primary-school	Secondary-school				
	Middle U5MR countries (26–94) **Median**	**106.7**	**92.5**	**99.0**	**99.1**	**51**	**44**	**82**	**90**
65	Madagascar	103.0	83.8	94.4	69.8	..	18	62	300ˣ
66	Ecuador	106.6	94.1	100.0	103.9	40	11ʸ	27	220ˣ
67	Papua New Guinea	103.0	63.6	80.9	53.3	4	..	34	1000
68	Brazil	108.5	96.2	91.7	..	65	..	73	154
69	Burma	106.0	..	..	..	5	21	97	135
70	El Salvador	106.8	92.0	..	..	47	19*	35	74
71	Dominican Rep.	106.4	98.7	..	..	47	87*	98	56ˣ
72	Philippines	106.0	98.8	101.1	104.8	33	49	..	80
73	Mexico	107.2	95.7	98.3	96.4	48	..	..	92
74	Colombia	107.3	97.8	102.6	102.0	51ˣ	6ʸ	51	126
75	Syrian Arab Rep.	105.9	56.6	91.9	68.1	20ˣ	19*	37	280
76	Paraguay	107.7	93.4	97.7	96.8	39ˣ	61*	22	469
77	Mongolia	106.6	92.5ˣ	101.9	109.5	..	..	99	140ˣ
78	Jordan	106.1	72.4	100.0	97.5	26	52	75	..
79	Lebanon	106.8	80.2	90.5	98.2	53ˣ	..	45	..
80	Thailand	106.4	93.6	100.0*	100.0*	63	45	33	270
81	Albania	106.1	..	96.0	86.5	..	..	..	..
82	China	104.3	68.3	86.4	71.1	71	..	..	44
83	Sri Lanka	105.3	91.2	97.1	111.7	57	44	87	90
84	Venezuela	109.1	96.6	99.1	122.0	49ˣ	..	82	65
85	United Arab Emirates	107.0	65.5ˣ	101.3	122.6	..	..	96	..
86	Guyana	107.7	97.9	..	..	35ˣ	93*	93	104ˣ
87	Argentina	110.0	99.0	100.9	113.6	74	..	..	85ˣ
88	Malaysia	106.5	81.5	99.0	101.9	51	48*	82	59
89	Panama	105.7	98.9	101.1	112.5	59	29*	83	90
90	Korea, Dem. Rep. of	109.8	..	..	..	..	..	99	41
91	Korea, Rep. of	109.8	91.7ˣ	100.0	94.9	70	..	..	34
92	Uruguay	109.7	101.1ˣ	98.2	..	..	13ʸ	..	56ˣ
93	Mauritius	107.6	86.5	102.1	92.5	75	55	84	52
94	Romania	108.3	..	99.0	102.7	58ˣ	..	99	175
95	Yugoslavia	108.3	88.7	100.0	95.2	55ˣ	..	..	27
96	USSR	112.5	..	..	..	..	..	100	..
	Low U5MR countries (25 and under) **Median**	**109.1**	**95.9**	**100.0**	**104.3**	**71**	**..**	**99**	**11**
97	Chile	109.3	99.0ˣ	98.1	109.5	43	..	95	55
98	Trinidad and Tobago	107.8	97.9	103.4	106.8	55ˣ	60ʸ	90	81ˣ
99	Jamaica	108.0	103.3ˣ	103.2	107.1	52	50*	89	102
100	Kuwait	106.5	82.9	96.5	94.1	..	2*	99	18
101	Costa Rica	107.5	98.9	101.2	110.3	68	90*	93	26
102	Portugal	110.8	89.9	98.0	118.6	70ˣ	..	..	15
103	Bulgaria	107.7	..	99.0	101.1	76ˣ	..	100	22
104	Hungary	110.9	..	102.1	101.4	74ˣ	..	99	28
105	Poland	111.5	..	100.0	108.2	75ˣ	..	..	12
106	Cuba	105.0	100.0ˣ	100.0	107.3	60	..	..	31
107	Greece	106.1	90.7	101.1	96.6	..	..	..	12
108	Czechoslovakia	110.8	..	101.0	..	..	..	100	8
109	Israel	105.6	95.9	103.1	109.6	..	..	99	5
110	New Zealand	109.1	..	100.0	102.4	..	..	99	20
111	USA	110.5	..	100.0	99.0	68	..	100	9
112	Austria	110.2	..	98.0	105.2	71	..	..	11
113	Belgium	109.9	..	102.2	103.2	81	..	100	10
114	German Dem. Rep.	108.7	..	98.0	96.3	..	..	..	17
115	Italy	109.5	98.0	100.0	98.6	78ˣ	..	..	13
116	Singapore	108.0	84.0	100.0	104.3	74	90	100	11
117	Germany, Fed. Rep. of	109.7	..	100.0	102.7	..	..	..	11
118	Ireland	107.9	..	100.0	111.0	60ˣ	..	..	7
119	Spain	108.6	94.8	100.0	103.4	51ˣ	..	96	10ˣ
120	United Kingdom	109.0	..	100.0	104.8	83	..	98	7
121	Australia	109.7	..	100.0	103.2	67ˣ	..	99	11
122	Hong Kong	107.5	85.3	100.0	109.1	72ˣ	90	..	6
123	France	111.4	..	100.0	108.8	79ˣ	..	..	13
124	Canada	110.0	..	98.1	101.0	73	..	99	2
125	Denmark	108.6	..	101.0	99.0	63ˣ	..	..	4
126	Japan	107.5	..	100.0	102.1	57	..	..	15
127	Netherlands	109.7	..	103.5	97.1	78	..	..	5
128	Switzerland	109.6	..	..	..	70ˣ	..	..	5
129	Norway	109.9	..	100.0	105.3	71ˣ	..	100	4
130	Finland	111.5	..	99.0	115.8	80ˣ	..	..	5
131	Sweden	108.7	..	102.1	111.4	78	..	100	4

TABLE 8: BASIC INDICATORS ON LESS POPULOUS COUNTRIES

#		Under 5 mortality rate		Infant mortality rate (under 1)		Total population (millions) 1986	Annual no. of births/infant and child deaths (0–4) (thousands) 1986	GNP per capita US $ 1985	Life expectancy at birth (years) 1986	% adults literate male/female 1985	% of age group enrolled in primary school male/female 1983–86
		1960	1986	1960	1986						
1	Gambia	361	287	205	166	0.7	32/9	230	37	36/15	92/58
2	Djibouti	..	..	..	152*	0.4	../..	480ˣ	..	15*/9*	../..
3	Equatorial Guinea	315	219	188	129	0.4	17/4	180ˣ	46	../..	../..
4	Swaziland	227	178	152	120	0.7	32/6	670	50	70/66	112/110
5	Vanuatu	..	..	..	101*	0.1	../..	880	..	57ˣ/48ˣ	../..
6	Comoros	216	132	128	81	0.5	21/3	240	52	56ˣ/40ˣ	107ˣ/78ˣ
7	Sao Tome and Principe	..	91ʸ	..	74ʸ	0.1	../..	320	..	73ˣ/42ˣ	../..
8	Maldives	..	91	..	68*	0.2	../..	290	..	83ˣ/82ˣ	../..
9	Cape Verde	213	91	143	65	0.3	11/1	430	61	61/39	111/105
10	Solomon Islands	..	..	..	44*	0.3	../..	510	..	../..	../..
11	St. Christopher/Nevis	..	..	..	41*	(.)	../..	1550	65*	../..	../..
12	Dominica	..	..	..	40*	0.1	../..	1150	77ʸ	../..	../..
13	Qatar	239	43	145	33	0.3	11/(.)	16270	71	51ˣ/51ˣ	120/121
14	Saint Vincent	..	..	..	33*	0.1	../..	850	..	../..	../..
15	Samoa	..	..	..	33*	0.2	../..	660	..	../..	../..
16	Suriname	96	39	70	31	0.4	11/(.)	2580	69	90/90	136/130
17	Antigua and Barbuda	..	..	..	30*	0.1	../..	2020	70ʸ	../..	../..
18	Bahrain	208	34	130	28	0.5	14/(.)	9420	70	79/64	113/110
19	Fiji	98	33	71	27	0.7	21/1	1710	70	90/81	129/128
20	Bahamas	..	..	..	23*	0.2	../..	7070	..	../..	../..
21	Belize	..	..	..	23*	0.2	../..	1190	..	../..	../..
22	Saint Lucia	..	..	..	18*	0.1	../..	1240	73ʸ	../..	../..
23	Seychelles	..	21*	..	17*	0.1	../..		70*	56ˣ/60ˣ	103ʸ/102ʸ
24	Cyprus	36	17	30	15	0.7	13/(.)	3790	75	96ˣ/83ˣ	100*/100*
25	Grenada	..	..	..	14*	0.1	../..	970	66ʸ	51*/49*	../..
26	Brunei Darussalam	..	..	..	12	0.2	../..	17570	..	85ˣ/69ˣ	../..
27	Barbados	91	15	74	11	0.3	5/(.)	4630	73	../..	113/108
28	Malta	42	14	37	11	0.4	7/(.)	3310	73	86/82	100/94
29	Luxembourg	41	11	33	8	0.4	4/(.)	14260	72	../..	101/99
30	Iceland	22	7	17	6	0.2	4/(.)	10719	77	../..	97/100

Note: nations are listed in descending order of their 1986 under-five mortality rates

Footnotes to Tables

Table 1:
Basic Indicators

Sierra Leone	Primary enrolment	1982
Angola	GNP per capita	1980
	Primary enrolment	1982
Chad	GNP per capita	1982
Central African Rep.	Primary enrolment	1982
Mauritania	Primary enrolment	1982
Burundi	Adult literacy	1982
Sudan	Adult literacy	1986
Tanzania, U. Rep. of	Adult literacy	1986
Uganda	Primary enrolment	1982
Oman	Adult literacy	1982
Egypt	Household income	1974
Peru	Household income	1972
Saudi Arabia	Adult literacy	1982
Turkey	Adult literacy	1984
	Household income	1973
Iraq	GNP per capita	1980
Brazil	Household income	1972
Mongolia	Adult literacy	1982
Venezuela	Household income	1970
United Arab Emirates	Adult literacy	1975
Argentina	Household income	1970
Malaysia	Household income	1973
Panama	Household income	1973
Korea, Rep. of	Adult literacy	1982
Uruguay	Adult literacy	1975
Romania	GNP per capita	1983
USSR	GNP per capita	1980
Chile	Adult literacy	1984
Jamaica	Adult literacy	1980
Costa Rica	Household income	1971
Portugal	Household income	1973–4
Bulgaria	GNP per capita	1980
Cuba	Adult literacy	1981, age 10+
Czechoslovakia	GNP per capita	1980
German Dem. Rep.	GNP per capita	1980
Ireland	Household income	1973

Table 2:
Nutrition

Sierra Leone	Breast-feeding	1978
Ethiopia	Breast-feeding	1977
Somalia	Breast-feeding	Urban only
	Malnutrition	Age 0–6
Burkina Faso	Wasting	1978
Angola	Breast-feeding	1976, duration not stated
Yemen	Breast-feeding	1979
	Malnutrition	1979
	Wasting	1979
Yemen, Dem.	Wasting	1978
Nepal	Breast-feeding	1976
	Malnutrition	1976
	Wasting	1974
Bangladesh	Breast-feeding	1976
Sudan	Breast-feeding	1979
Bolivia	Breast-feeding	1977
	Malnutrition	1979
Haiti	Breast-feeding	1979
	Wasting	1978
Uganda	Malnutrition	Between 70% and 80% standard weight for height
		Less than 70% standard weight for height
Zaire	Breast-feeding	1975–6
Cameroon	Breast-feeding	1978
Togo	Breast-feeding	1977
	Wasting	1977
Egypt	Breast-feeding	1978
	Malnutrition	1978, pre-school population
	Wasting	1978
Morocco	Malnutrition	1971
Congo	Malnutrition	Age 0–15
Kenya	Breast-feeding	1978
	Wasting	1979
Tunisia	Malnutrition	1975
Guatemala	Breast-feeding	1978
Papua New Guinea	Malnutrition	1978, age unspecified
	Wasting	1975
Ecuador	Malnutrition	Age 0–6
Brazil	Malnutrition	Age 0–17
Burma	Malnutrition	Age 0–3
Dominican Rep.	Malnutrition	Rural only
Philippines	Breast-feeding	1978
Mexico	Breast-feeding	1976
Syrian Arab Rep.	Breast-feeding	1978
Jordan	Wasting	1975
Paraguay	Breast-feeding	1979
Thailand	Breast-feeding	1979
	Wasting	1978

continued over

Sri Lanka	Breast-feeding	1975	
	Wasting	1976	
Venezuela	Breast-feeding	1977	
Malaysia	Breast-feeding	1974	
Korea, Rep. of	Breast-feeding	1974	
Panama	Breast-feeding	1979	
	Malnutrition	1975, age unspecified	
Trinidad and Tobago	Breast-feeding	1977	
Jamaica	Breast-feeding	1976	
Costa Rica	Breast-feeding	1976	
	Malnutrition	1978	
Hungary	Breast-feeding	1975–6	
Poland	Breast-feeding	1977	
Hong Kong	Breast-feeding	1974	
Canada	Breast-feeding	1978	
Netherlands	Breast-feeding	1975	

Table 3:
Health

Afghanistan	Maternal mortality	1978
Sierra Leone	Immunization	1984
Malawi	Maternal mortality	1975
Ethiopia	Immunization	Age 1–2
Guinea	Measles	Age 1–5
Mozambique	Drinking water	1980
	Maternal mortality	Hospital data only
Burkina Faso	Maternal mortality	Hospital data only
Niger	Tuberculosis, polio and measles	Age 0–3
	DPT	Age 0–5
Chad	Drinking water	1975
Central African Rep.	Drinking water	1975
	Immunization	Age 1–2
Senegal	Maternal mortality	1975
Mauritania	Immunization	1984
Nepal	Maternal mortality	1979
Benin	Tetanus	1984
	Maternal mortality	Hospital data only
Tanzania,U. Rep. of	Health service	1978
	Maternal mortality	Institutional deaths only
Bolivia	Maternal mortality	1973–77
	Measles	Age 1–5
Gabon	Immunization	Age 1–2
Oman	Drinking water	1980
Cameroon	Drinking water	1975
	Maternal mortality	1975, Hospital data only
Togo	Immunization	Age 0–3
	Maternal mortality	1977
Côte d'Ivoire	Tuberculosis, DPT, polio and measles	1984, Age 0–3
	Tetanus	1984
Ghana	Immunization	Age 0–2
	Maternal mortality	Hospital data only
Lesotho	Immunization	Age 0–2
Peru	Measles	Age 1–5
Libyan Arab Jamahiriya	Maternal mortality	1978
Congo	Polio	2 doses only
Kenya	Maternal mortality	1977
Zimbabwe	Drinking water	1980
	Maternal mortality	1979, Hospital data only
Honduras	Measles	Age 1–5
	Maternal mortality	1979
Algeria	Immunization	Age 1–2
Guatemala	DPT, polio	2 doses only
Saudi Arabia	Immunization	Age 1–2
Nicaragua	Maternal mortality	1978
Turkey	Drinking water	1977
	Attended births	1983
	Maternal mortality	1974–5
Botswana	Attended births	1986
Madagascar	Maternal mortality	1979
Ecuador	Measles	Age 1–5
	Tetanus	1984
	Maternal mortality	1978
Brazil	Polio	2 doses only
	Measles	Age 1–5
El Salvador	Polio	2 doses only
Dominican Rep.	DPT	2 doses only
	Polio	Age 0–3
	Measles	Age 9–24 months
	Maternal mortality	1978
Mexico	Polio	Age 0–4
	Measles	age 1–5
Colombia	Tetanus	1983
Syrian Arab Rep.	Drinking water	1980
Mongolia	Maternal mortality	1978
Jordan	Tuberculosis	1983
Lebanon	Drinking water	1980
China	Drinking water	1980
	Immunization	12 months for 23 provinces
		18 months for 5 provinces

Venezuela	Tuberculosis	1984	
United Arab Emirates	Drinking water	1980	
Guyana	Maternal mortality	1977	
Argentina	Measles	Age 1–5	
	Maternal mortality	1979	
Korea, Rep. of	Immunization	1984	
	Measles	age 1–5	
Uruguay	Polio	2 doses only	
	Measles	Age 1–5	
	Tetanus	1984	
	Maternal mortality	1978	
Trinidad and Tobago	Measles	Age 1–2	
	Tetanus	1983	
	Maternal mortality	1977	
Jamaica	Drinking water	1975	
Kuwait	Drinking water	1975	
Hungary	Tuberculosis	1984	
Poland	DPT, polio	1984	
Cuba	Polio	2 doses only	
Greece	Tuberculosis	1983	
New Zealand	DPT, polio	1983, 2 doses only	
	Measles	Age 1–5	
USA	DPT, polio	1983	
	Measles	Age 1–5	
Austria	Tuberculosis, DPT and polio	1984	
	Measles	1983	
Belgium	DPT, polio	1984	
Italy	Tuberculosis, polio	1984	
Singapore	Measles	Age 1–5	
Spain	Maternal mortality	1979	
United Kingdom	Immunization	1984	
Australia	Measles	1983	
Denmark	Immunization	1984	
Japan	Immunization	1984	
	Polio	2 doses only	
	Measles	Age 1–5	
Netherlands	DPT	1984	
Norway	Tuberculosis	1983	
Finland	Immunization	1983	
Sweden	Immunization	1983	
	DPT	DT only	

Table 4:
Education

Sierra Leone	Primary enrolment	1982	
	Primary completion	1976	
	Secondary enrolment	1982	
Angola	Primary enrolment	1982	
Niger	Primary completion	1977	
Chad	Primary completion	1975	
Central African Rep.	Primary enrolment	1982	
	Secondary enrolment	1982	
Liberia	Secondary enrolment	1980	
Bhutan	Primary completion	1978	
Burundi	Adult literacy	1982	
Sudan	Adult literacy	1986	
Tanzania, U. Rep. of	Adult literacy	1986	
Bolivia	Primary completion	1976	
Haiti	Primary completion	1978	
Uganda	Primary enrolment	1982	
	Primary completion	1978	
	Secondary enrolment	1982	
Zaire	Primary completion	1976	
Oman	Adult literacy	1982	
	Primary completion	1977	
Iran (Islamic Rep. of)	Primary completion	1969	
India	Primary completion	1978	
Côte d'Ivoire	Primary completion	1978	
Ghana	Primary completion	1977	
Saudi Arabia	Adult literacy	1982	
Turkey	Adult literacy	1984	
Colombia	Primary completion	1973	
Paraguay	Primary completion	1977	
Mongolia	Adult literacy	1982	
	Primary completion	1978	
Venezuela	Primary completion	1978	
United Arab Emirates	Adult literacy	1975	
Argentina	Primary completion	1975	
Korea, Rep. of	Adult literacy	1982	
Uruguay	Adult literacy	1975	
Chile	Adult literacy	1984	
Jamaica	Adult literacy	1980	
Portugal	Primary completion	1974	
Cuba	Adult literacy	1981, Age 10+	

continued over

Table 5:
Demographic Indicators

Afghanistan	Contraceptive prevalence	1971–2
Senegal	Contraceptive prevalence	1978
Yemen	Contraceptive prevalence	1979
Sudan	Contraceptive prevalence	1978–9, North only.
Cameroon	Contraceptive prevalence	1978
Turkey	Contraceptive prevalence	1978
Iraq	Contraceptive prevalence	1974
Colombia	Contraceptive prevalence	1980
Syrian Arab Rep.	Contraceptive prevalence	1978
Paraguay	Contraceptive prevalence	1979
Lebanon	Contraceptive prevalence	1971
Venezuela	Contraceptive prevalence	1977
Guyana	Contraceptive prevalence	1975
Romania	Contraceptive prevalence	1978
Yugoslavia	Contraceptive prevalence	1976
Trinidad and Tobago	Contraceptive prevalence	1977
Portugal	Contraceptive prevalence	1979–80
Bulgaria	Contraceptive prevalence	1976
Hungary	Contraceptive prevalence	1977
Poland	Contraceptive prevalence	1977
Italy	Contraceptive prevalence	1979
Ireland	Contraceptive prevalence	1970
Spain	Contraceptive prevalence	1977
Australia	Contraceptive prevalence	1970
Hong Kong	Contraceptive prevalence	1977
France	Contraceptive prevalence	1978
Denmark	Contraceptive prevalence	1975
Switzerland	Contracpetive prevalence	1980
Norway	Contraceptive prevalence	1977–8
Finland	Contraceptive prevalence	1977

Table 6:
Economic Indicators

Mali	Poverty level	1975
	Government expenditure	1986
Ethiopia	Poverty level	1976
Angola	GNP per capita	1980
Niger	Poverty level	1975
Chad	GNP per capita	1982
	Poverty level	1976
Rwanda	Poverty level	1975
Bhutan	GNP per capita growth rate	1981–5
Bangladesh	Government expenditure	1985–6
Sudan	Poverty level	1975
Bolivia	Poverty level	1975
Lao People's Dem. Rep.	Government expenditure	1984–5
Zaire	Poverty level	1975
Iran (Islamic rep. of)	GNP per capita growth rate	1980–3
Egypt	Poverty level	1978
Saudi Arabia	Government expenditure	1986
Iraq	GNP per capita	1980
	Poverty level	1975
Romania	GNP per capita	1983
	GNP per capita growth rate	1980–84
USSR	GNP per capita	1980
Jamaica	Government expenditure	1984–5
Bulgaria	GNP per capita	1980
Czechoslovakia	GNP per capita	1980
German Dem. Rep.	GNP per capita	1980

Table 7:
Women

Afghanistan	Contraceptive prevalence	1971–2
Afghanistan	Maternal mortality	1978
Sierra Leone	Primary enrolment	1982
	Secondary enrolment	1982
Malawi	Maternal mortality	1975
Mozambique	Maternal mortality	Hospital data only
Burkina Faso	Maternal mortality	Hospital data only
Angola	Primary enrolment	1982
Central African Rep.	Primary enrolment	1982
	Secondary enrolment	1982
Senegal	Contraceptive prevalence	1978
Liberia	Secondary enrolment	1980
Yemen	Contraceptive prevalence	1979
Nepal	Maternal mortality	1979
Burundi	Adult literacy	1982
Benin	Tetanus	1984
	Maternal mortality	Hospital data only
Sudan	Adult literacy	1986
Sudan	Contraceptive prevalence	1978–9, North only.
Tanzania, U. Rep. of	Adult literacy	1986
Tanzania, U. Rep. of	Maternal mortality	Institutional deaths only
Bolivia	Maternal mortality	1973–77
Uganda	Primary enrolment	1982
	Secondary enrolment	1982

Oman	Adult literacy	1982
Cameroon	Contraceptive prevalence	1978
Cameroon	Maternal mortality	1975, Hospital data only
Togo	Maternal mortality	1977
Côte d'Ivoire	Tetanus	1984
Ghana	Maternal mortality	Hospital data only
Libyan Arab Jamahiriya	Maternal mortality	1978
Kenya	Maternal mortality	1977
Zimbabwe	Maternal mortality	1979, Hospital data only
Saudi Arabia	Adult literacy	1982
Nicaragua	Maternal mortality	1978
Turkey	Adult literacy	1984
Turkey	Contraceptive prevalence	1978
Turkey	Attended births	1983
	Maternal mortality	1974–5
Iraq	Contraceptive prevalence	1974
Botswana	Attended births	1986
Madagascar	Maternal mortality	1979
Ecuador	Tetanus	1984
	Maternal mortality	1978
Dominican Rep.	Maternal mortality	1978
Colombia	Contraceptive prevalence	1980
Colombia	Tetanus	1983
Syrian Arab Rep.	Contraceptive prevalence	1978
Paraguay	Contraceptive prevalence	1979
Mongolia	Adult literacy	1982
Mongolia	Maternal mortality	1978
Lebanon	Contraceptive prevalence	1971
Venezuela	Contraceptive prevalence	1977
United Arab Emirates	Adult literacy	1975
Guyana	Contraceptive prevalence	1975
Guyana	Maternal mortality	1977
Argentina	Maternal mortality	1979
Korea, Rep. of	Adult literacy	1982
Uruguay	Adult literacy	1975
	Tetanus	1984
	Maternal mortality	1978
Romania	Contraceptive prevalence	1978
Yugoslavia	Contraceptive prevalence	1976
Chile	Adult literacy	1984
Trinidad and Tobago	Contraceptive prevalence	1977
Trinidad and Tobago	Tetanus	1983
	Maternal mortality	1977
Jamaica	Adult literacy	1980
Portugal	Contraceptive prevalence	1979–80
Bulgaria	Contraceptive prevalence	1976
Hungary	Contraceptive prevalence	1977
Poland	Contraceptive prevalence	1977
Cuba	Adult literacy	1981, Age 10+
Italy	Contraceptive prevalence	1979
Ireland	Contracpetive prevalence	1970
Spain	Contraceptive prevalence	1977
Australia	Contraceptive prevalence	1970
Hong Kong	Contraceptive prevalence	1977
France	Contraceptive prevalence	1978
Denmark	Contraceptive prevalence	1975
Switzerland	Contracpetive prevalence	1980
Norway	Contraceptive prevalence	1977–8
Finland	Contraceptive prevalence	1977

Table 8:

Basic Indicators on less populous countries

Djibouti	GNP per capita	1981
Equatorial Guinea	GNP per capita	1981
Vanuatu	Adult literacy	1979
Comoros	Adult literacy	1980
	Primary enrolment	1980
Sao Tome and Principe	Under 5 mortality	1984
	Infant mortality	1984
	Adult literacy	1980
Maldives	Adult literacy	1977
Dominica	Life expectancy	1984
Qatar	Adult literacy	1981
Antigua and Barbuda	Life expectancy	1984
Saint Lucia	Life expectancy	1984
Seychelles	Adult literacy	1971
	Primary enrolment	1982
Cyprus	Adult literacy	1976
Brunei Darussalam	Adult literacy	1982

Definitions

Under-five mortality rate: annual number of deaths of children under 5 years of age per 1,000 live births

Infant mortality rate: annual number of deaths of infants under one year of age per 1,000 live births.

GNP: gross national product. Annual GNPs per capita are expressed in current United States dollars. GNP per capita growth rates are annual average growth rates that have been computed by fitting trend lines to the logarithmic values of GNP per capita at constant market prices for each year of the time period.

Life expectancy at birth: the number of years new-born children would live if subject to the mortality risks prevailing for the cross-section of population at the time of their birth.

Adult literacy rate: percentage of persons aged 15 and over who can read and write.

Primary and secondary enrolment ratios: the gross enrolment ratio is the total number of children enrolled in a schooling level – whether or not they belong in the relevant age group for that level – expressed as a percentage of the total number of children in the relevant age group for that level. The *net* enrolment ratio is the total number of children enrolled in a schooling level who belong in the relevant age group, expressed as a percentage of the total number of children in that age group.

Income share: the percentage of private income received by the highest 20% and lowest 40% of households.

Low birth-weight: 2,500 grammes or less.

Breast-feeding: either wholly or partly breast-feeding.

Child malnutrition: mild or moderate: between 60% and 80% of the desirable weight-for-age; *Severe:* less than 60% of the desirable weight-for-age.

ORS: oral rehydration salts.

Prevalence of wasting (acute malnutrition): the percentage of children with greater than minus two standard deviations from the 50th percentile of the weight-for-height reference population, i.e. roughly less than 77% of the median weight-for-height of the United States National Center for Health Statistics reference population.

Access to health services: percentage of the population that can reach appropriate local health services by the usual local means of transport in no more than one hour.

DPT: diphtheria, pertussis (whooping cough) and tetanus.

Maternal mortality rate: annual number of deaths of women from pregnancy related causes per 100,000 live births.

Children completing primary school: percentage of the children entering the first grade of primary school who successfully complete that level in due course.

Crude death rate: annual number of deaths per 1,000 population.

Crude birth rate: annual number of births per 1,000 population.

Total fertility rate: the number of children that would be born per woman, if she were to live to the end of her child-bearing years and bear children at each age in accordance with prevailing age-specific fertility rates.

Absolute poverty level: that income level below which a minimum nutritionally adequate diet plus essential non-food requirements is not affordable.

Contraception prevalence ratio: percentage of married women age 15–44 currently using contraception.

ODA: official development assistance.

Debt service: the sum of interest payments and repayments of principle on external public and publicly guaranteed debts.

Main Sources

Under-five and infant mortality: United Nations Population Division and United Nations Statistical Office

Total population: United Nations Statistical Office and United Nations Population Division

Child population: United Nations Population Division

Births: United Nations Population Division

Infant and child deaths: United Nations Population Division and UNICEF

GNP per capita: World Bank

Life expectancy: United Nations Population Division

Adult literacy: United Nations Educational, Scientific and Cultural Organization (UNESCO)

School enrolment and completion: United Nations Educational, Scientific and Cultural Organization (UNESCO)

Household income: World Bank

Low birth-weight: World Health Organization (WHO)

Breast-feeding: World Health Organization (WHO)

Child malnutrition: World Health Organization (WHO) and UNICEF Field Offices

Wasting (acute malnutrition): World Health Organization (WHO)

Food production and calorie intake: Food and Agriculture Organization of the United Nations (FAO) and World Bank

Access to drinking water: World Health Organization (WHO)

Access to health services: World Health Organization (WHO)

Immunization: World Health Organization (WHO) and UNICEF field offices

ORS: World Health Organization (WHO)

Births attended: World Health Organization (WHO)

Maternal mortality: World Health Organization (WHO)

Radio and television receivers: United Nations Educational, Scientific and Cultural Organization (UNESCO)

Crude death and birth rates: United Nations Population Division

Fertility: United Nations Population Division

Urban population: United Nations Population Division

Contraceptive prevalence: United Nations Fund for Population Activities (UNFPA)

Inflation: World Bank

Absolute poverty level: World Bank

Expenditure on health, education and defence: World Bank

Official development assistance: Organisation for Economic Cooperation and Development (OECD)

Debt service: World Bank

UNICEF Headquarters
UNICEF House, 3 UN Plaza, New York, NY 10017, USA

UNICEF Geneva Headquarters
Palais des Nations, CH-1211 Geneva 10, Switzerland

UNICEF Regional Office for Eastern and Southern Africa
P.O. Box 44145, Nairobi, Kenya

UNICEF Regional Office for Central and West Africa
P.O. Box 443, Abidjan 04, Côte d'Ivoire

UNICEF Regional Office for the Americas and the Caribbean
Apartado Aéreo 75 55, Bogotá, Colombia

UNICEF Regional Office for East Asia and Pakistan
P.O. Box 2–154, Bangkok 10200, Thailand

UNICEF Regional Office for the Middle East and North Africa
P.O. Box 811721, Amman, Jordan

UNICEF Regional Office for South Central Asia
73 Lodi Estate, New Delhi 110003, India

UNICEF Office for Nigeria
P.O. Box 1282, Lagos, Nigeria

UNICEF Office for the People's Republic of China
12 Sanlitun Lu, Beijing, China

UNICEF Office for Australia and New Zealand
G.P.O. Box 4045, Sydney NSW 2001, Australia

UNICEF Office for Japan c/o United Nations Information
Centre, 22nd Floor, Shin Aoyama Building Nishikan
1–1, Minami – Aoyama 1-Chome, Minato-ku Tokyo 107, Japan